How to Start, Run and Grow a Successful Gas Station Business

A Complete Guide to Gas Station Business

A to Z

By

Shabbir Hossain

How to Start, Run, and Grow a Successful Gas Station Business

Copyright (C) 2015 CSB Academy Publishing Co.

All rights reserved. In accordance with the U.S. Copyright Act of 1976, the scanning, uploading, and electronic sharing of any part of this book without the permission of the publisher is unlawful piracy and theft of the author's intellectual property. If you would like to use material from this book (other than for review purposes), prior written permission must be obtained by contacting the publisher. Thank you for your support of the author's rights.

CSB Academy Publishing Co.

Cover designed

By

Angie Anderson

2nd Edition

Contents

ABOUT THE AUTHOR 8
    About the 2nd Edition 9

PREFACE 12

PART I 15

CHAPTER 1: WHY A GAS STATION? 16
    Gas Stations as an Effective Business Model 16
    Is the Gas Station Business Right for You? 21
    Decide How You're Going To Get There 35

CHAPTER 2: PICKING YOUR LOCATION 40
    Finding Properties for Sale 40
    Gauging Property Cycles and Real Estate Values 44
    Assessing Prospective Properties 49
    Picking the Best Location for Your Business 55

CHAPTER 3: TO BUY OR LEASE A GAS STATION BUSINESS 67
    Buying A Gas Station Business 67
    Leasing A Gas Station Business 73
    The Politics of Developing Commercial Real Estate Sites – The Fine Print for Any Business Owner Buying their Business Property 74

CHAPTER 4: DUE DILIGENCE 79
    Inspecting the Site 83
    Property Assessment Strategies 92
    Assessing the Business Aspect 101

CHAPTER 5: FINANCING **104**

FINANCING ANALYSIS POINTERS FOR COMMERCIAL PROPERTY PURCHASES 106

NOI, DSCR, LTV, AND THE CAP RATE 111

NET OPERATING INCOME (NOI) 112

DEBT SERVICE COVERAGE RATIO (DSCR) 113

LOAN TO VALUE (LTV) 115

CAPITALIZATION RATE (CAP RATE) 115

TYPES OF LOANS AND LENDERS 119

COMMERCIAL LOANS BASED ON CREDIT 120

PURCHASING OR RE-FINANCING WITH A HARD MONEY MORTGAGE 120

DOCUMENTS TO PROVIDE TO HARD MONEY LENDERS 122

BRIDGE LOANS 123

THE IMPORTANCE OF APPRAISALS TO YOUR FINANCING OPTIONS 125

APPRAISAL OF MARKET VALUE 127

FACTORS TO CONSIDER SPECIFIC TO GAS STATIONS 129

CHAPTER 6: CLOSING THE DEAL **132**

INVENTORY VALUATION AT COST 132

WRAPPING YOUR HEAD AROUND THE CLOSING 133

THE JOURNEY FROM NEGOTIATION TO CLOSING 136

LETTER OF INTENT 137

OPTIONS CONTRACTS 144

SPLIT-FUNDING 145

FLOATING SELLER-HELD MORTGAGES 147

PARTIAL RELEASE AGREEMENT 147

ENGAGING YOUR SELLER 148

WORKING OUT THE FINE PRINT.. 150

CHAPTER 7: THE LEGAL STUFF **155**

TYPES OF COMPANIES 155

    A. Corporations *156*

    B. Limited Liability Company (LLC)... *157*

    C. Partnership *158*

INCORPORATING YOUR BUSINESS 160

UNDERSTANDING STATE AND LOCAL REGULATORY LICENSES................ 162

    Regional Regulations that May Apply *166*

    State Regulations that May Apply... *166*

    Federal Regulations (for Employers) *169*

    Underground Storage Tanks Registrations..................................... *169*

RESELLERS CERTIFICATE FROM STATE DEPARTMENT OF REVENUE 177

EMPLOYMENT IDENTIFICATION NUMBERS... 178

YOU (OR YOUR COMPANY) AS AN EMPLOYER 178

BASIC PAPERWORK FOR EMPLOYERS.. 179

PAYROLL WITHHOLDING REQUIREMENTS... 180

FRINGE BENEFITS 181

UNEMPLOYMENT INSURANCE 182

WORKERS' COMPENSATION 182

HEALTH PLANS 183

BASIC RECORD KEEPING 184

PART II 186

CHAPTER 8: BECOMING ORIENTED POST-PURCHASE 187

FIGURING OUT YOUR FIRST MOVE 189

BRANDED VS. UNBRANDED GASOLINE 191

DETERMINING YOUR OPENING DAY 193

CHAPTER 9: MARKET RESEARCH AS THE FIRST STEP TO MANAGEMENT 195

QUESTIONS YOU NEED TO ASK (AND ANSWER) REGULARLY 196

ORGANIZING MARKET RESEARCH INFORMATION 200

MARKETING TOOLS AND SCHEDULES 200

ANALYZING MARKETING DATA AND ACTING ON IT 201

CHAPTER 10: YOUR FIRST DAYS OF BUSINESS: PUTTING A PLAN INTO ACTION 204

PRE-OPENING CHECKLIST 204

FIRST DAY CONTINGENCIES 207

ESTABLISHING YOUR DAILY SCHEDULE 209

PROMOTE YOUR STORE WITH A SMILE TO GET PEOPLE THROUGH THE DOOR 210

CHAPTER 11: BUILDING YOUR BUSINESS THROUGH MARKETING 213

BUILD YOUR IMAGE 215

DIVERSIFY YOUR EFFORTS 216

STAY ORGANIZED AND DILIGENT 218

LOGOS, MOTTOS, AND SLOGANS 219

THE FIRST 30 SECONDS – WHAT SALES SHOULD LOOK LIKE IN A GAS STATION 220

CHAPTER 12: HIRING THE RIGHT PEOPLE 222

ESTABLISH JOB DESCRIPTIONS AND POSITIONS 226

CALCULATING WAGES AND BENEFITS 230

CREATING EMPLOYEE APPLICATIONS AND CONTRACT DRAFTS 231

MANAGING YOUR STAFF 233

CHAPTER 13: UNDERSTANDING AND MAXIMIZING SALES 234

KEEPING UP APPEARANCES 237

INVENTORY MANAGEMENT 239

LOSS PREVENTION 241

KEEPING THE BOOKS (ACCOUNTING) 247

CONCLUSIONS AND APPENDIX 248

SAMPLE BUSINESS PLAN 250

FURTHER RESOURCES 269

SOME USEFUL BUSINESS BOOKS 269

SOME USEFUL BUSINESS WEBSITES AND ONLINE TOOLS 270

About the Author

Shabbir Hossain graduated from the University of South Alabama in 1994 with a Bachelor of Science degree in Business Marketing. He started his first business the year before graduating – Byte 1 Computers and Software. Eighteen months later, the business was closed.

After moving to Tampa, Florida, Shabbir leased a BP gas station from a local company, launching his first gas station venture. Shortly after that, he applied to the BP Oil Corporation to become an authorized dealer and was ultimately selected to lease and operate either one of two stations. One was in Greenville, SC, and the other one in Mobile, AL.

Having lived in Mobile before, Shabbir chose to move back to Mobile and worked hard to build up a relationship with the local community there. Before long, Shabbir owned seven gas stations, and his secured yearly sales were over $5 million consistently.

The key behind Shabbir's rapid success was mostly common sense marketing, promotion, and merchandising – the type of strategies that so many gas station owners overlook, along with practical location management strategies.

Today, Shabbir shares his knowledge of gas station business management via the CStore Business Academy (http://gasstationbusiness101.com) website and blog.

Shabbir recently started a new weekly audio podcast show called "Gas Station Business 101 Podcast." In this podcast, he talks about the recent changes, opportunities, and challenges of today's gas station business. You can find his show in many podcasting directories like iTunes, Stitcher, blubrry, and Tunein.

About the 2nd Edition

First, let me offer my sincere apologies to all the readers out there that read my book and found typos and spelling mistakes. As I went through the book and had someone to look it over, we sure did find a few errors. To my weak defense, I am not a writer and never was one. I remember in college, I didn't even want to take English 102 until my graduation semester because I was afraid I would fail that course.

In 2011, after helping a few friends start their gas station business, I began thinking maybe there are others out there that can use the same help. With that thought in mind, I started writing a few pages each night after dinner. After about 9 months, I had something that was nearly 180 pages long. Then, I hired an editor online who I thought was a pro, but it turned out that she was certainly not.

Long story short, I went back and tried to fix many of the errors she made. I had hired her to fix my errors and, in the end, I am fixing hers. With the help of my daughter, who was an English major, I believe we were able to fix all of the issues.

I am sure some of you may still find one or two typos, so I will ask for your forgiveness ahead of time.

This book may seem long, especially when you read through the sections where I talk about various zoning, plats, and UST regulations. If these do not apply to you, just skip to the next chapter.

If you visit my blog at http://www.gasstationbusiness101.com/resources/, you will find some very useful tools of the trade. You can even download and use them for your own business.

Please feel free to send me any questions you may have about this book or about a business you are trying to acquire. Whatever the case, just know that I am here to help.

You can visit my blog and ask me questions there. Sign up for my newsletter to receive upcoming gas station operations help documents.

Lastly, an announcement about my new podcast, "Gas Station Business 101 Podcast." You can find my episodes on many podcast hosting services including iTunes, Stitcher, TuneIn Radio, Blubrry, and many other podcast directories.

Preface

The American dream is still alive and well. We may be taking its pulse more frequently than we did in the past, but we know, for now, for the foreseeable future, there is little reason to question its vibrancy.

Walk down the street. Drive down your nearest highway. Look left, look right, look straight ahead. Everywhere, there is evidence of America's promise, the gift of hopes and dreams, which took form with our founding fathers.

At the heart of the American dream, beating loud and strong, is the notion that any man or woman can go into business for themselves.

It's only really the details of the dream that have changed. Not all that much is different. Recently, more people may be looking to start a business online, working with little more than a website and a logo.

The risks and odds against success with an online business have sustained the popularity of certain brick-and-mortar businesses.

Among the most American, the most workable, and even still the most popular business models today is that of the gas station.

Gas stations, whether on highways, in small towns, or in cities, are the quintessential American businesses still found all around the country. As a small business opportunity, gas stations represent excellent investment opportunities for anyone looking to establish a business.

The goal of this book is to outline the steps necessary to go about buying or building-up a gas station business from scratch. In the first few chapters, I will talk about what makes a gas station a viable business for most situations.

We will discuss how you can get started as a gas station business owner, and what you need to know to ensure that your business has a solid foundation, financially and legally.

From chapter eight onwards, I will talk about ways that you can work to grow your business over time. I will outline key marketing and sales strategies that have proven successful with the gas station model and with other similar business models.

I will also offer some ideas on how you can go about creating a long-term plan for your business, including marketing and strategic components. This will ensure that your business is not just successful but you, as the business owner and presumptive manager, are taking steps to ensure the overall efficiency and maximum profitability of your business based on your location, your marketing options, your target market, your current customer base, and your sales model.

Complementing the information in this book, which is based on extensive research of business principles and strategies, as well as analysis of the gas station business models, are numerous case studies, sample documents, and templates for you to work with as an aspiring gas station business owner.

When you have worked your way through this book, taking notes and assessing the information as it might best be applied to your situation, you will have a solid understanding of what it takes not only to establish a gas station business but also what it takes to really grow a successful gas station business. Consider strategies to build a customer base, upsell to each and every customer who walks onto your lot, and establish a reputation for customer service and solid business principles.

Shabbir Hossain
C STORE BUSINESS ACADEMY

Facebook: **CsbAcademy** Twitter: **CSB_Academy**

LinkedIn: **CstoreBusiness Academy**

Part I
Establishing Your Gas Station Business

Chapter 1: Why a Gas Station?

Before you do anything to establish yourself as a gas station business owner, before you even think about setting foot on a gas station lot to consider the business potential, you need to understand exactly why a gas station business is the way to go. You have to understand, not only from a general business perspective but also from a personal perspective, exactly why a gas station is the right business for you – if, in fact, it really is.

Gas Stations as an Effective Business Model

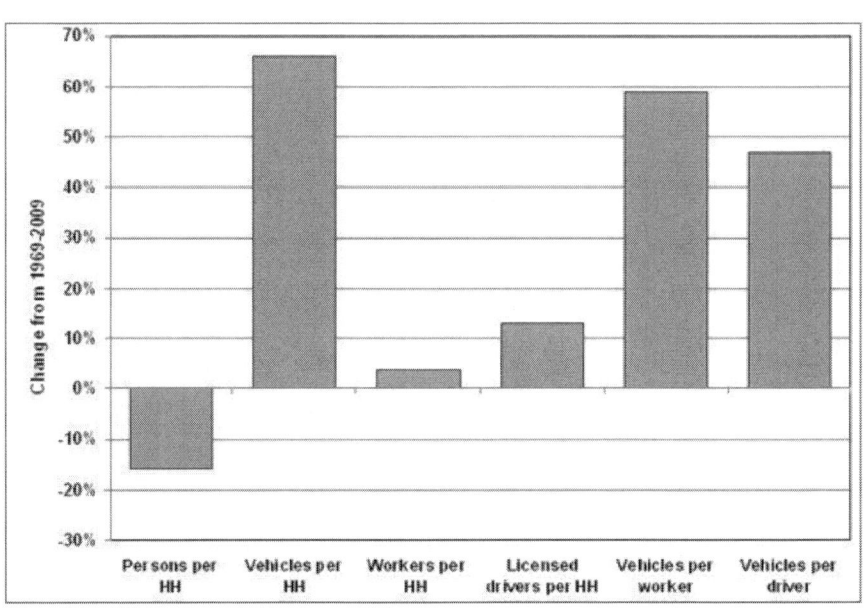

Figure 1 http://www1.eere.energy.gov/vehiclesandfuels/facts/2010_fotw618.html

Why is a gas station a good business model for just about any aspiring businessperson? The question, really, is why not?

At the end of the day, America is a convenience-loving, car-hugging country. Owning your own car is the key to independence in the United States. Americans love their cars.

A couple of statistics to keep in mind: approximately 68% of American respondents in a recent survey indicated that they own a car, SUV, or truck. About 55% of the cars we own are an American brand, too. Both men and women equally have a tendency to be emotionally attached to their cars, picking cars that fit their character.

The number of cars per household is also pretty high these days. As of April 2010, the number of vehicles per household was calculated at 2.66 cars per household.

Certainly, this means that people need a lot of gasoline. Ever since Henry Ford invented the automobile, our appetite for fuel has steadily grown to a total of about 697 gallons of fuel per vehicle per year (in 2006).

Gas stations are not just "gas stations." They are not just there to provide gasoline to drivers who need to fill up their tanks.

	1969	1977	1983	1990	1995	2001	2009	Percent change 1969–2009
Persons per household	3.16	2.83	2.69	2.56	2.63	2.58	2.66	-16%
Vehicles per household	1.16	1.59	1.68	1.77	1.78	1.89	1.92	66%
Workers per household	1.21	1.23	1.21	1.27	1.33	1.35	1.26	4%
Licensed drivers per household	1.65	1.69	1.72	1.75	1.78	1.77	1.87	13%
Vehicles per worker	0.96	1.29	1.39	1.40	1.34	1.39	1.52	59%
Vehicles per licensed driver	0.70	0.94	0.98	1.01	1.00	1.06	1.03	47%

In fact, the American gas station is a basis for the classic corner store – the type of store that is found on just about every street corner, in just about every neighborhood across the United States. In essence, the gas station, like a corner store type business, is as American as apple pie.

A typical neighborhood gas station carries not only gasoline but also over 2,000 everyday items from a gallon milk to a bottle of ketchup.

In a nutshell, the convenience store industry includes 152,000 stores as of December 2013, according to NACS. The combined annual revenue from these stores runs to about $700 billion, and most of the c-store, or convenience store, owners are individual owner-operators. Many owners actually own multiple locations, enjoying, therefore, multiple income streams from a single business concept.

The convenience store industry, of course, includes many of the establishments that are gas station/c-store combinations. This means that the information we just reviewed – the part about the $700 billion industry and the majority of these businesses having an individual owner - applies quite readily to the gas station business model that is the focus of this book.

Although the profitability of individual stores depends on competitive pricing, effective merchandising, and the ability to secure high-traffic locations - all of which we will discuss in this book.

The breakdown of sales is also worth considering. Major products sold in convenience stores (the combination gas station and convenience stores) usually include fuel (representing about 70% of sales), groceries and cigarettes (representing about 10% of sales), and beer (representing about 5% of sales).

The average annual revenue per worker in a US gas station is about $700,000, and fuel for motor vehicles accounts for 80% of industry sales. Major products sold include regular unleaded gas (about 60% of fuel sales) and diesel fuel (about 30%). Gas stations also sell unleaded mid-grade and premium unleaded gas and bring in a good portion of revenue that way. On average, establishments that are strictly truck stops sell more diesel fuel than the regular gas stations.

In addition to maintaining an inventory of snacks, soft drinks, and candy products (especially those that double as convenience stores), many gas stations also provide auto repair bays, tire, and battery retailing, and even on-site car washes. Truck stops tend to offer food, phones, showers, and lounges for truckers and travelers. Some of the larger gas stations offer all of these services to patrons as well. What it really comes down to is the innovation of the station/store owner and the particulars of the business site.

The reason that gas stations provide such an excellent business model comes down to perhaps two key factors. The first is that gas stations are essentially recession-proof businesses. Since the economic slowdown and the recession, we have seen yet more proof that people continue to need gas for their cars and milk, as one of the staple products sold in gas station convenience stores. Secondly, the gas station and gas station/convenience store industry is one of the very few industries that have seen a growth in numbers since 2008.

Is the Gas Station Business Right for You?

You should now have a pretty clear idea of why gas stations present a viable business model in general terms.

Basically, they make a profit, and they are likely to make a profit under just about any general economic circumstances. In a recession, that is, when people are looking to cut back on their spending, causing many businesses to lose revenue, gas stations and especially gas station-c-stores are going to continue to have fairly steady revenue, simply because people still need (and will buy) their gas, tobacco, soda, and perhaps even their milk.

What about you, though?

Although gas stations offer a great business model, there's little actual value starting a business about which you have minute personal interest.

There are numerous adages that extol the importance of being involved in a business (or a job, for that matter) about which you are passionate and invested. If you can't get excited about the idea of owning a gas station, chances are, it's not for you.

On the other hand, if the model interests you and you can see the potential to make something out of it, then you have probably already found your niche.

Once you have decided that at least the idea of having a gas station business is amenable to you, the thing you really need is a plan. Not a business plan at this point, although you will need that at a later point.

What we're talking about here is a personal financial plan, where you sit down with a piece of paper and write down what and how much is available to you, how much you can borrow, and what you have as collateral.

Your personal roadmap should be as simple as a list or a series of statements about what you want.

Regardless of how you decide to lay out your plan, you should explore your goals in the following areas:

1. *In Your Personal Life* – Whether you're single, in a relationship, or married (or anywhere in between), what are your goals for your personal life and how do you intend to meet them? An obvious one is to think about your significant other, whether you want to find someone to fit this role or that you have someone already.

    Determine what you want in terms of your personal life as this will help you create the strength you need to go to work. If you already have your personal life worked out in terms of who's in it (i.e., you're married or in a relationship), be prepared to work out how your relationship might be impacted by the first few months of setting up your gas station business. How involved is your partner going to be? How are you going to deal with potential stresses or tensions in your relationship if you have to go through a period of working abnormally long hours or having relatively little money to spare?

2. *In Your Family Life* – Especially when you are starting a new business, one that may be fairly time intensive in the beginning, having the support

of family makes a big difference. The support of your family is something that you also have to temper. It's often said that working with, lending money to, or accepting money from family members is not a good idea and, generally speaking, that is true. You may have one or two family members that want to invest in your business.

Exercise caution and be extra scrupulous in your decision-making about such things. For the most part, you should look to your family to stay grounded and confident in yourself. Make sure you set aside time for your family, too; to visit your parents more regularly or to call your siblings at least once a week. Small efforts like these will help to reinforce a positive relationship with your family, helping you to prepare to move on to your future of business success.

3. **In Your Career** – How often do we get sidetracked when it comes to our career goals? Considering that business ownership was at least in the realm of possibility as far as goals go, take a look at your professional life as a whole and see where you are and where you might want to go. Business ownership is a great thing, but it neither has to define nor limit your professional scope.

Assuming you do the legwork to set up your business to function properly, you may not need to have much in the way of everyday, hands-on involvement. Instead, you may be able to look to other projects – perhaps more gas stations, more convenience stores, a new type of business, perhaps a regular 9 to 5 job - just to keep you grounded or to move you up the career ladder, amassing experience along the way.

If you have some aspect of your professional life that you haven't addressed in a while, or some personal goals for a career that you haven't achieved, factor these into your game plan for personal development on your way to being a successful business owner.

4. ***In Your Intellectual Development*** – Knowledge is food for the mind just as spirituality is good for the soul. You don't have to be a straight A-student to enjoy learning new things, particularly when you're an adult. You don't have to take a course to develop your intellect, either. You could simply visit your local library and commit to reading one book a month or every two weeks, depending on what your schedule allows. Alternatively, you could take up a mental game like bridge or chess.

Numerous studies have shown that actively exercising the mind improves memory and helps to prevent the degenerative diseases of old age, such as Alzheimer's. Your mind is like a muscle. You need to exercise it regularly to keep it in shape, and the more you exercise it, the stronger it becomes. A strong mind is an excellent asset to have as you embark on a quest to create millions. It's almost essential. Find a mental activity you enjoy, set a schedule, and stick to it. You'll gain more confidence in yourself and your abilities as you test yourself in this way. Not to mention, there are plenty of things you can do to work on your intellectual development while at the same time working on your straight knowledge of the business.

There are whole libraries of books out there on the subject of business and related issues such as marketing and sales. Most of the best business people in the world, the best entrepreneurs, set out to find a way to change the rules of the game. With the gas station business model, you have a solid and time-tested industry to work within. Why not read up on business and marketing as a way to expand your intellectual horizons but also work on your business plans?

5. ***In Your Spiritual Development*** – No rule says you have to be religious to be spiritual. The two are not mutually exclusive, and sometimes, in fact, one has little to do with the other. Spirituality can often be more about having a certain consciousness of the world at large. Whatever you believe or don't believe about the particulars, there are things in this world that we as human beings haven't explained.

    There are also times when we need to take a step back from the world and from the everyday grind of our daily experiences. Whether you decide to take a ten-minute walk every day to focus your thoughts, or you sign up for a yoga class and start practicing meditation, set a goal to develop your spirituality as you set a goal to develop your intellect. Again, as you become more in touch with this aspect of who you are, you'll increase your general confidence, your self-awareness, and your strength as an individual. All of these are to steps to achieving your goal of becoming a successful business owner because they provide you with an important means of obtaining some perspective in your life.

6. ***In Terms of Your Physical Well-Being*** – To work long days, even just to be productive as a

business owner, to make important decisions with a clear head, you need to be in good physical health. Improving your physical well-being, however, does not mean that you should look to a Hollywood actress or actor as your role model. Healthy, physical well-being is achieved by eating a balanced, healthy diet with enough of the right calories in addition to vitamins, minerals, and fiber. The right amount of exercise is what you feel comfortable with.

Most physicians and fitness experts suggest at least three half-hour workouts per week for the average, healthy adult. To begin work on your physical well-being, examine how you currently live. Do you eat enough fruits and vegetables per day? Do you drink enough water? When it comes to exercise, find an activity that isn't too strenuous. The best type of exercise for maintaining health is aerobic exercise – walking, swimming, and jogging – and this is generally what you should start out doing. Establish a schedule to address your physical well-being as a goal of developing yourself.

Have fun. Moderate exercise is a great way to reduce stress as you will create all-natural stress-reducing hormones called endorphins. You'll almost certainly feel more relaxed and focused as you start integrating a physical regime and good eating habits into your routine. Lowering stress, enhancing focus, and building endurance will help you be more effective in your business. Not to mention these habits make a much happier you.

The best way to have a plan for yourself is to take these categories I have just mentioned and write out one to three goals for each.

These goals should be SMART goals, which I will talk about shortly. They should be at least somewhat related to each other and to what we are assuming to be a broader, longer-term goal for you – creating a successful gas station business.

You are not the only thing that needs a plan, though. Your business needs direction, as well. Imagine you are about to go on a real trip. You're going on an adventure to climb Mount Everest. You have a general idea of where you want to go. You want to get to the top of the mountain, the highest point in the world.

It's a fine plan to start with, but you can't really embark on such a trip without an actual map of where you are going. You have to create a plan of how you're going to get to the summit.

When creating a successful business is your goal, you need a detailed plan of how you're going to achieve this. It is comprised of various different elements. There are several major steps involved in becoming a successful business owner and generating a relatively large income – assuming you want to support yourself and your family and have some general flexibility in your life.

Let's say it again for emphasis: You need a plan in place to create and sustain a successful business.

As you may know already, the best way to deal with this is to write a comprehensive business plan.

You need a business plan to start your own business. It is common sense. Most business start-ups require a financial investment of some sort in the beginning. Even if all you're doing is buying a business card, a website domain, and a couple of packs of pencils, you are still spending money on your business venture. You need to make sure the money comes back to you. A business plan will take care of that.

Since you are starting a gas station business, the need for a comprehensive and professional looking business plan is crucial. Without a well-written, carefully thought out, and professional-looking business plan to back you up, you are unlikely to get much assistance from prospective investors. Many sellers or owners of gas stations (those you might approach to buy or lease a gas station) are very unlikely to take you seriously if you can't show them a solid business plan.

Unfortunately, most people don't have a clue about where to begin writing their business plan. Sometimes, this is because they haven't really thought enough about their business idea. If you haven't thought about how to turn your idea into a reality, then you probably have to spend more time brainstorming before you start trying to write up your plan. Otherwise, you may belong to the group of people who have simply never seen a business plan. You can visit my blog at http://www.gasstationbusiness101.com and take a look at a business plan I have that I once used as part of a loan package for a bank loan.

Although everyone is different, most business plans have the following components:

1. **Executive Summary** – This section describes the basic idea behind the company. For all intents and purposes, this section is the general introduction to the plan. A lot of companies choose to explain the reasons for starting the company in the first place. They may also provide a brief summary of the history of the particular industry they are entering.

2. **Objectives** – Presented as bullet points, the objectives of a company are outlined in a business plan so that it is clear to whoever is reading the plan precisely what the goals of the individual and the team might be.

3. **Market Segment Analysis** – This section is basically an in-depth review of customers and consumers. It describes those who you intend to target with your business.

4. **Product/Service Information** – Here, you need to explain the importance of the product or service you're offering. This section generally includes a review of the product or service, pointing out why they are different from everything else on the market and why it can be deemed that there is a substantial need.

5. **Marketing Strategies** – This section explains how the business will be advertised to various audiences. Most business plans provide a general outline of marketing strategies that are further explained in a marketing plan.

6. **Sales Strategies** – These are crucial to the success of a business, so every business plan includes a section devoted to explaining how sales will be achieved. A number of key questions are generally

answered: Who will handle the daily operation of the business? How will you grow sales? How will you do the accounting and bookkeeping for the business?

7. **Personnel Information** – Business plans generally include a review of the company structure and planning. An important aspect of this is the company staff. Personnel with positions of authority, whether they are managers or executive assistants, can have an important role to play in the development and ultimate success of a company. Career experience, education level, assigned responsibilities, and relevant skill sets are generally outlined in this section. Sometimes resumes for personnel are included in the plan.

8. **Financial Summary and Projections** – Although financial projections for start-up businesses are generally based on guesswork, they are an important element of a business plan. It is vital to outline a plan of the money that will go into the company, and it is also important to try to determine how much money will come out of it. Gradually, financial summaries and projections can be updated as more information is collected, and the company begins to generate income.

There are plenty of good books that outline how to write a business plan. A general web search will also produce a range of relevant results. It's important to put time and effort into your plan to get it as water-tight and close to perfect as you can. Your plan is a blueprint for your company, and there are a lot of different working parts to consider.

Of course, your business plan is not the only roadmap or blueprint you need. Your business is a crucial part of your effort to make millions, but it is by no means the only element. You, as an individual, need to develop a blueprint for your personal development.

To be happy, centered, and focused are essential qualities to becoming rich; it is next to impossible to be successful if you don't first feel successful. It's not about accepting what you've already achieved as all you can achieve.

Feeling successful is about recognizing the positives in your life. It's about realizing that you have already achieved a great deal. You can achieve more, certainly, but you've already achieved a lot. Outline a plan to recognize your track record. Start on a path of self-discovery. Try to become more self-aware. As you do, you'll learn amazing things about yourself that will reinforce your strengths and help to improve your weaker areas.

The more you can do to prepare yourself mentally for entering into the business world, for taking on the responsibility of managing a gas station, the more likely you are to succeed at it.

Decide How You're Going To Get There

A classic technique for goal setting and management is the SMART system. It's used by many of the world's top organizations to assess the nature of your goals.

According to the SMART program, your goals should be:

- Specific - Have you clearly defined your goal?
- Measurable - How do you know if you are making progress?
- Achievable - Is your goal really achievable? Be ambitious but honest.
- Rewarding - Is your goal something you are willing to make a sacrifice for?
- Timely - Is your goal achievable in a meaningful timeframe?

How do you begin to achieve your lifetime goals?

Once you have set your lifetime goals, life coaching experts recommend setting a twenty-five-year plan of smaller goals that you should complete if you are to reach your lifetime plan.

Once you have a twenty-five-year plan, you should set a five-year plan, a one year plan, a six-month plan, and a one month plan.

Establish progressively smaller goals that you need to achieve to meet your lifetime goals.

Each set of goals should be based on the previous plan.

Set a daily to-do list of things that you should do to work towards your lifetime goals.

The steps you take during the first days and through the first months may be very simple. These goals may be to read certain books and otherwise gather the information that will help you achieve your goals. In the beginning, you should work to improve the quality and realism of your goal setting. To stay on track, you should regularly review your plans, and make sure that they continue to fit the way you want to live your life.

When you've decided on your first set of plans, establish a habit to review and update your to-do list daily. Review your longer-term plans periodically and modify them to reflect your changing priorities and experience.

When it comes to setting your goals, keep this process in mind:

1. Write out each goal as a positive statement.

2. Be precise when you write your goals, record specific dates, times, and amounts so that you can measure your achievement.

3. Set priorities so that each of your goals has a priority ranking. This helps you to avoid feeling overwhelmed by too many goals and directs your attention to the most important ones.

4. Write goals down regularly as this helps you keep focused on them.

5. Keep low-level goals you work towards daily small and achievable. Keeping goals small and incremental gives you more opportunities to reward yourself.

6. Take care to set goals over which you have as much control as possible. If you keep your goals focused on personal performance, then you can keep control over

the achievement of your goals and draw satisfaction from them.

7. It is important to set goals that you can achieve, in full recognition of your own desires and ambitions.

8. Do not set goals too low; the best goals are just slightly out of your immediate grasp, but not so far that there is no hope of achieving them.

As you achieve your goals, short-term and long-term, be sure to enjoy the satisfaction of having done so. Absorb the implications of the goal achievement. Monitor and revel in your progress towards your life goals. Reward yourself.

As you set up your business and take on the responsibility of managing it, you are going to need to stay motivated through the ups and downs. Hopefully, there are going to be considerably more 'up' days than 'down' days.

Another important step is to keep reviewing your goals. Check the following:

- Are your goals too easy to achieve? Make your next goals harder.

- Are your goals taking too long to achieve? Make your next set of goals a little easier to achieve.

- Have you learned something that might lead you to change other goals? If the answer is yes, change the relevant goals.

- Have you noticed a deficit in your skills? Set goals to resolve this.

Keep in mind that failure to meet goals does not matter. As long as you learn from your failures and your mistakes (think of Edison and how many times he failed at creating inventions), failure is not an issue.

As you learn lessons, incorporate them into your goal-setting program and remember that your goals will change as you mature. Adjust your goals regularly to reflect this growth in your personality. If any one of your goals is no longer attractive to you, let them go and let go of the attached emotions.

Goal setting should bring you real pleasure, satisfaction, and a sense of achievement.

Chapter 2: Picking Your Location

Finding the right gas station and actually getting it – buying it – is going to be tough. You are looking at a very competitive market when it comes to finding an optimum location. For every store, there are also at least ten willing buyers out there. These potential buyers are people who will have done all their homework, submitted it on time, and pulled together everything they need to buy when the owner is ready to commit. You cannot afford to hesitate once you know you've found the one. You have to be fast, decisive, and ready to sign. You have to be faster than everyone else.

Here's the catch. You don't want to end up with the wrong business, either. There's no point in moving at a breakneck speed only to find out, several months down the line, perhaps, that you've bought yourself a business with a problem – a money drainer that is going to do nothing but cause you headaches.

Do your homework first, and then get ready to act fast. That is the order of business you need to aim for.

Finding Properties for Sale

The first thing you need to do, of course, is to find out what properties are up for grabs in your target community.

Fortunately, there are a few ways to go about finding a station for sale.

Lesson number one is that not every one of them you find is a money-making one. If it is making money, then why are they selling it?

Your first test is to figure out whether there are good reasons for the sale that have nothing to do with the fact that the business is not making money.

You have to be a good listener and use your judgment. Do some double-checking to see if they are telling you the truth as far as why they are selling it.

There may be a couple of key components to the asking price of a station as well. You should make a point to find out what they are in each case. Most likely they will include the price of the real estate if the land is included in the sale, a certain "goodwill" part, sometimes referred to as the "blue sky" money, and perhaps also the cost of inventory at the day of sale.

Depending on the particulars of the deal and price, you may find that there is a certain amount of merchandise in the store and gasoline in the tank the day you take over the store. If so, these will probably also be factored into the price you pay for the property.

As far as actually finding gas stations properties for sale, though there are four main ways to do it:

1. **Through local business brokers**. Check the local phone book under real estate to find business brokers. There are few national companies like Coldwell.

2. **Through local realtors**. Most realtors have a commercial wing where they list businesses and commercial properties for sale. It's best to contact a reputable real estate company and ask to speak to someone in their commercial department.

3. **Through the local Newspaper "Businesses for Sale" ads**. Make a point of checking one or two of your local newspapers.

4. **Through the web**. This is my second choice after the local business brokers. There are many online business broker and commercial listing sites.

It's always a good idea from a research perspective to research website listings. One site you may want to take a look at, which pulls all of the MLS listings from local real estate companies, is https://www.loopnet.com. You can find anything and everything commercial for sale in any locality anywhere on this site and get a good idea of the property markets in your target areas.

You can also try https://www.bizbuysell.com. This site only pulls listings from business brokers around the country and not from real estate companies.

There are few specialty sites that deal only with gas stations for sale and nothing more. One prime example is https://www.nrc.com.

In addition to these options, there are even a few more localized specialty brokers and websites to checkout. You may find one more suitable for your city and state than another, but it may take some time and some networking to identify them. One example would be https://www.gasstationsusa.com. This site focuses on the state of Florida.

Last, but not the least, by any means, is my favorite way to find a station. This method is how I got into this business 20 years ago. I contacted the local oil companies that supply fuel to the stations around town.

They also may be the ones who own some of those stores. So, it is a good idea to find out what local oil companies are in your area. Typically, in a small to mid-size city, there may be anywhere from 5 to 15 jobbers representing Exxon to Shell and all companies in between. Keep in mind that some of them may represent more than one fuel brand.

When I was getting started, I called a few local reps and asked for an appointment with one of the key employees. With a foot in the door, I explained that I was in the market to find a gas station that I could operate and make a living with.

Remember to be very polite but professional. They are not your business brokers but probably the owners of big oil jobber firm.

Your goal is to establish yourself as an honest, hard-working individual, willing to take direction from them. If they like you, they may help you find a store, and you get control of a business by spending very little money.

Gauging Property Cycles and Real Estate Values

Picking your location comes down to a few different factors, including what properties are actually available to you. In addition to figuring out which larger companies may be interested in going into business with you – if you demonstrate yourself to be a committed and capable individual – you are going to need to be able to find and either buy or lease a suitable property to establish your gas station business.

The focus of this chapter and the few that follow is very much conducting due diligence. When you've finished reading through this section, you should have a clear idea of the research you are going to need to conduct to get a strong handle on the best property – the best site – for your gas station business.

Before we go into detail, however, let's look at property cycles and the effect that they have upon the value of the real estate. The last thing you want to do with your gas station business is to start off on the wrong foot, picking a business site that could based on its value or any other related factor, essentially cripple your operation from the start.

First of all, the pattern of a so-called, idealized "property cycle" uses an adaptive expectation framework. Although there are relatively few books published dealing with commercial real estate alone, you would probably be hard-pressed to find a single book about gas stations, specifically. It won't be hard to find a book about property cycles, should this strike you as an attractive past time. Yet, the bulk of the literature focuses on identifying a broad pattern among property cycles rather than focusing on the nitty-gritty specifics.

Generally, the stages and points of a property cycle are as follows:

1. The first stage is an upturn in business and development. This is the first point of the property

cycle. Typically at a time of low-interest rates and the availability of high capital, there is a rise in economic activity, and an increased desire to make use of the real estate. This stage is generally achieved after a period of comparatively low levels of development. Vacancy rates continue to fall, and rents continue to rise. So-called "investor optimism" increases as capitalization rates fall. These are the effects of lower interest rates, lower expected risk, and higher expected rental growth.

2. The second stage of the ideal property cycle involves the realization of the expected profitability of the new development. The new development that began during the first phase of the cycle continues and raises the value of land in the affected area. A real estate boom is in place as lending is now offered to those interested in undertaking what are considered to be speculative development projects. A lag is noted between the point at which construction starts and development is completed, nonetheless, what this means, primarily, is that there is a limited new supply of real estate reaching the market. As demand is still high and as yet unmet, rents and capital values continue to increase.

3. The third phase of the cycle is the point at which the equilibrium for supply and demand of available property is met and surpassed. The business enters a downturn on its upward spiral as overbuilding starts to become a problem. Real interest rates are rising by

this point, primarily as a response to the real estate boom. In reaction, business cycles turn downwards. The demand and absorption of new space has now leveled off and is beginning to fall. The new development that had begun in the previous two phases has reached the market at last, but since demand has fallen now, the vacancy rates have started to rise, and rental growth is definitely faltering.

4. The fourth phase of the cycle is the point at which capitalization rates rise along with real interest rates. The principle issue is evident in poorer growth prospects. Capital values are falling, and as in the first stage, the valuation of the properties is relatively delayed.

5. The fifth phase of the cycle is adjustment, as the fall in demand for new real estate space finally comes in line with a peak in supply as new developments are available. Vacancy rates are now rising above the equilibrium level, and rents are falling in response to the gradual adjustments.

6. In the fourth phase, developers cannot generate income to cover interest payments. The completed developments and lower capital values have essentially put a stop to refinancing at this point.

7. Slump demand and development have become relatively low, and vacancy rates have risen well above equilibrium levels.

8. The next cycle is in the works.

In most instances, the demand for property is determined by the need to have a property with which to conduct a range of activities. The need to occupy the property is generally established by the need to produce goods and services, for which there is a pronounced demand. The usual measure of this demand is related to output, expenditure, or employment in the appropriate sectors of the economy. Examples of services include employment offices, retail sales, manufacturing output, and warehousing activity in various industrial and commercial contexts.

When it comes to assessing properties, it is important to know that square feet are the units by which office, industrial, and retail properties are typically measured. Often, measurements are in either "gross square feet" or "net square feet."

Unlike properties used for straightforward businesses, apartments, hotels, and self-storage facilities are usually measured in square feet. Most often, however, commercial properties put to this use are measured based on the number of units or rooms. A standard apartment complex with 100,000 square feet would be better described as a property with 800 units. A hotel with 80,000 square feet would be more accurately described as a property with 300 rooms.

You will learn as well that the address, city, or state location of a property is rarely used to describe its location. The most common identifier for location is the submarket location of the property. In most locations, it is a specific region that determines the submarket.

Assessing Prospective Properties

In terms of your investments and investment strategies, however, you are going to need to look beyond the basic details of the properties you are interested in. You are going to have to extend your comfort zone to take you through some of the most complex aspects of commercial real estate understanding. First of all, you are going to have to understand how a real estate insider goes about picking their properties, as the only sure way for you to make your investments a success is going to involve you following the same types of principles and pointers that experienced investors use.

The first element you are going to have to familiarize yourself with is the listing service. The local board of realtors in your area, as well as other real estate groups that deal with the transfer of properties, will have sources of information that they use to post a list of properties that are available for sale (the MLS).

Your first step in assessing possible properties for your gas station business is always going to involve checking with a realtor to find out more about their list or a specific property on their list.

You are going to want to make real estate listings in all of those free magazines that advertise real estate a part of your daily reading. You should definitely be working regularly to stay up to date with properties in your area that are changing hands, even if you are not interested in investing at a particular time.

To get your hands on the most useful listings of real estate in your area, the good news is that you don't have to go very far. Most magazines are free, and they are available in your local grocery store, restaurants, and a whole host of other buildings frequented by tourists.

When people visit an area of the country or a part of the world that is unfamiliar to them, one of the first things they like to do is get a handle on the real estate market. That's why real estate magazines – the free ones with the property listings – are posted where they are. You should find a few listings and plenty of information relevant to your gas station business plan.

Aside from the magazines we've mentioned, you can also take a look at the real estate section of your local newspaper. Often this section is provided weekly, and it should include a section somewhere detailing recent sales, including the names of both the buyer and the seller, the price that the property sold for, and perhaps, if you're lucky, a few other tidbits about the deal. As you get more involved in the buying or leasing process, you will probably want to start keeping a file of clippings and notes about properties that you've been tracking or that have interested you.

FSBO (For Sale By Owner) is going to be another important source of information for you. The way to pronounce the word, by the way, is "fizz-boa." What it refers to is the "for sale by owner" properties - the types of properties for sale that are not listed by realtors or other brokerage firms but offered exclusively by the owner.

You will often come across these types of properties by accident, and you should certainly try calling the phone number posted on the sign or announcement to find out more about the property. Meeting with people to discuss features of properties is going to be an important part of your learning curve. You will quickly familiarize yourself with the property market in your local area if you are prepared to immerse yourself in it this way.

The next step will be to examine the active listings from your local real estate brokerage firms. The term "active listings" is used to refer to properties that realtors are actively working on. Generally, this means that the properties in question are not sold. They may, however, be sales pending, expired, closed, or canceled. The active list refers to those properties that are currently on the market. The close listings are generally interesting because when you go to find out about these, you will be able to seize useful information about the property.

Most experienced investors find the expired listings for real estate extremely interesting. There are listings of properties that have not sold, and the original listing has expired. Often, these properties will be relisted at a lower price in the hopes of finally attracting a buyer, or better yet, the property owner may be giving up hope. These properties become fair game for anyone with the patience to track the owner down and determine for themselves why the property did not sell. If you are working with a realtor, ask them to show you expired listings.

Another point of call for the very savvy investor is the local tax assessor. These professionals, more often than not, will maintain a detailed list of property records for their local community. Tax assessors often hold county-level positions, however, so contacting these professionals tends to open up a whole wealth of information about local properties that would otherwise have been inaccessible to you.

For every transaction that takes place relating to real estate, there is always some paperwork to be filed. At the office of the tax assessor, there will be public information on property transfers and mortgages. If you're particularly lucky, your local tax assessor may be regularly publishing the information online. Regardless, if you pay your local tax assessor's office a visit, you will be directed to people in the office who can walk you through computer programs, cards, or microfilm files on property information for the area.

When you're on the lookout for prospective properties, other resources you might consider are MapQuest (http://www.mapquest.com), Google Maps (http://www.googlemaps.com), and zoning maps. MapQuest and Google Maps, first of all, are two of several useful resources on the internet that you might consider regularly using to locate properties.

It goes without saying that many real estate listings can be found online as easily as they can be found in your local grocery store. Gas station facilities are even more specific of a thing to look for.

MapQuest and Google Maps are online mapping programs that allow you to develop a detailed map of just about any location in the United States. You can obtain aerial views of your location and based on this information, make assessments about property locations.

Zoning maps are available for each city. While these maps are not free, they are detailed enough to allow you to find virtually any property and get information about zoning restrictions relevant to their location. Using a magnifying glass to read the details, you can generally determine the different zoning codes that affect the location.

You will need to become familiar with the general codes for zoning, although it is simple enough. You will not have much trouble finding a relevant key, beside which under the heading "Residential Zoning," you will find a list that starts with codes such as R-1, R-1a, and so on. A brief description of what the code refers to should also be available.

Since it can be overwhelming – even for the experienced reader – to go through a long list of codes, you are strongly recommended to obtain a printed version of any zoning map you're interested in since you can then refer back to the print out to confirm details about a particular property that otherwise you may have missed.

Picking the Best Location for Your Business

When it comes to finding the best properties, the best locations for a gas station, from the various sources of information mentioned above, you should look to find properties with which you are relatively comfortable.

Ideally, any properties that you decide to shortlist for further investigation should have the following characteristics:

1. They should be near your residence or at least to a location that you know well.

2. They should offer a limited number of opportunities for development and use so that you can concentrate your interests.

3. They should be located within one area that you can easily oversee.

4. They should be located in an area that is well-defined, with high-traffic so that you can be sure of a steady stream of customers for your gas station business.

Close proximity indicates that a property should either be close to your home or close to the place where you work. You should be able to drive there easily either from your home, your office, or both.

When you are first inspecting a property to assess whether or not it is a viable base for your business, you should make several trips to view it. Ideally, on each trip, you should try to vary your route a little so that you provide yourself with ample opportunity to familiarize yourself with the surroundings of the area.

With your own interests still in mind, you should be looking to invest in prospective sites within a single area. Assuming you might expand your business to include multiple sites in the future, keeping all of your properties in one area, even while just considering properties. Staying within the same city or county jurisdiction, you not only reduce the amount of study and research you need to do, but you also ensure that you can become an expert in one set of rules and regulations that impact your business property.

Since your objective should be to become involved in the community that supports your business, you are going to be saving yourself a lot of work by identifying properties within one governing area.

The areas you operate in as a business owner should always be well-defined in the sense that they are either identified as a particular zone according to city or county mapping, defined in terms of natural boundaries or even just defined by market parameters.

The bottom line is that you are going to have to become an expert in the area and the community that you invest in. You are going to have to learn the basics of the community. You are going to need to learn how to operate effectively, identifying the appropriate tools to facilitate your investments; you are going to have to learn to keep detailed records of each important step you take. You will also have to conduct considerable research about commercial real estate deals that go through in the area.

About 90% of success in any form of commercial real estate investing is determined by how much you know about the area that you invest in. You need to understand the value of the property you invest in to support your business, which means that you need to start out by grasping the basics.

Although your primary business is going to be selling gasoline to customers, you still need to learn about the zoning and ordinances within your area of operation because they are going to impact your business and your prospects.

Part of this should be picked up naturally as you research specific properties, but you should also be prepared to go to meetings, including planning and zoning meetings for the area.

Be on the lookout for City Commission meetings. At these meetings, new development projects are discussed by community representatives. Listening to these discussions will help to keep you abreast of changes that are going to be affecting the area. Networking with the other people who attend these key meetings – the developers, their lawyers, and other experts – will also help you to get a better handle on your own projects.

Before you attend any meeting, however, you are going to need a few basic tools. First of all, you will need a city or county zoning map and a suitable book to help you decipher everything from the building and zoning ordinances and codes. Generally, these books are available from your city or county building and zoning department.

You'll also need a fairly comprehensive list of all of the principal characters involved in real estate projects; that means full names and contact information for your city or county commissioners, managers, and attorneys.

You will need contact information for the head of the building department, the head of the planning and zoning department, and the heads and members of your local planning and zoning board. If possible, you should also have the information for county commissioners just in case you need to contact them at some point. All of this contact information needs to be filed away appropriately so that you have easy access to it.

The good news is that most of this contact information is available for each of the departments of the bureaucracy. It should be relatively easy to obtain but, if you have any trouble, you should be able to resolve the problem simply by calling the office of your local city Mayor and asking their secretary to help you. If you mention that your principal purpose is to pursue investment in a facility suitable for the establishment of a gas station business, they should at least be able to refer you to someone who can help you get the information you need.

When it comes to keeping your records, your best bet is to have a digital copy and a paper copy of your collected data. For your names and addresses, invest in a good Rolodex but enter the information on an address book on your computer like Outlook Express so that you can save time when you need to address letters and envelopes. Backup all of your files on your computer as well. You never know when technology is going to fail you. It happens more often than most of us would like to believe.

Since you should also be looking to collect clippings and copies of published real estate information. It generally helps to have a filing cabinet or a folder to store information in as well. You should also invest in a digital camera so that you can keep a photographic record of every property you visit. Since digital cameras are so easily available, you should certainly consider investing in one of these. Nonetheless, printing out a copy of each of your photographs and writing down the date, property address, legal description, property owner information, and information about asking and sales prices should also become a part of your regular routine.

For your own properties, take pictures at regular intervals, at least once every year, so that you can keep an eye on the property maintenance efforts and its general state.

Research the activity of other investors in your community, or at least keep track of successful investment or business stories. You should establish a separate file to store information – notes and clippings – on each story.

The information you should take note of will include the names of the principal players, the location of the project development, and additional information about the particulars of each deal - whatever makes the story newsworthy and interesting to you.

For instance, if you keep track of the business news in your area, you will probably note when companies change hands or have special events. Being aware of this information will help you not only get a sense of how busy your local area really is, but it should also help you get a handle on the who's who aspect of things.

Research the following information about your community of focus:

- Building setback regulations by zoning codes.

- Building height allowances by the zoning code.

- Commissioner information by zone.

- Emergency plan information by zone.

- Strom and emergency shelter information.

- Fire codes relevant to each zone.

- Fire station information for each zone.

- Information on libraries and schools serving each area.

- School district information.

- Master plan information for transportation and traffic ways by zone.

- Hospital and emergency room information by proximity to each property.

- Public transportation information.

- Public park information by zone.

- Information on residential density restrictions by the zoning code.

- Utility upgrade plans by zone.

- Information on zoning codes.

All of this information should be at your fingertips, not because it is immediately relevant to your gas station business but because you cannot yet assess what is relevant and what is not. You need to get a sense of the area in which you are going to do business. That means you have to get a sense not only of the people – your target market, your base of customers – but also the properties surrounding what, in one way or another, is going to be your property.

To determine what investments are most appropriate for you, you should use this information to answer a series of questions to determine your interests. There are certainly two general types of gas station businesses, but there are numerous variations on those businesses that you can apply. Exactly what shape your gas station business takes is going to depend upon factors such as those we have just alluded to – the property value, the type of neighborhood, your customer/target market base, your interests, and your expertise.

To make the most of your investments, you should do the following:

1. Use your research to determine what zoning applies to these types of properties in your area.

2. Refer to the zoning maps that you have gathered in your research to determine the applicable zoning codes.

3. Highlight areas of the tone that match up to the zoning codes and regulations you have identified as being pertinent to your building types.

4. Look to identify and combine one or more local areas so that you can identify a minimum short-list of 100 properties to investigate and research for investment purposes.

5. Mark all applicable boundaries on your maps.

6. Start to look for information about the areas that you have identified for your initial investments. Search out notices about public meetings, homeowner meetings, and any other references to the areas that you have identified as being within your area.

Start researching the zoning regulations that apply to gas station facilities in your area. You should have all of this information readily available once you have secured the appropriate zoning and codebooks and additional information about zoning categories.

Don't be afraid to contact and consult with experts in the real estate and investment fields to determine whether your information and deductions are correct.

When you review your zoning maps and codes, don't hesitate to make copious notes on any relevant information. If you are working in an area that you know well – somewhere that you have either lived or worked for a while – you should be able to recognize various areas on your zoning map. Don't rule out areas too early on in the research process but keep your eye out for areas that do not appear appropriate for your business interests.

Using a yellow highlighter, or some other form of marker that won't impede your ability to read the details of the map, identify the areas on the map that you should start scouting out for appropriate gas station properties. You are going to want to do this to monitor things such as traffic volume, access to major roads in the area, competition from other gas stations, the proximity of grocery stores or convenience stores, and other potential factors that will be addressed a little later.

The next step, once you have identified such areas on your map, is to take a trip to see these locations in person.

Observe what is going on in the town. Look out for developments that are underway and certainly make a note of any properties that are either marked as for sale, for rent, or sold. For any such properties, determine the ownership. Investigate the history of ownership and the sales history for each property. For properties that are for rent, take a look at what the available property information tells you about the income potential for the area.

Use the rental market as a reference point to determine the value of the properties in the area.

Take a look at the value of other gas stations that have been on the market recently. If there are no facilities that have been bought or sold recently or even rented out, do a bit of research. Look through local records and determine approximately what value such properties have been given and, if the properties were bought or sold quite some time ago, make a comparison. Use other properties as a key to assess the relative values.

Use your gut instinct to determine what each area has working in its favor.

Scout out areas that appeal to you for whatever reason. You can spend quite some time driving around, discovering new areas that you have never noticed before. Be sure to make several copies of all of the maps that you get your hands on in the initial research phase because you are going to be making a lot of notes on these.

Chapter 3: To Buy or Lease a Gas Station Business

Whether you buy or lease, your first gas station business will depend entirely on your budget. A typical gas station costs anywhere from $250k all the way up to a couple of million dollars depending on factors such as location and age of the facility.

Although, I assume, throughout much of this book that you are actually going to go all-in with an investment, buying rather than leasing. It is important to be aware of all of your options, including the option to lease. You also want to make sure that you have relevant information if you decide to lease with an option to buy, for example.

In this chapter, we will explore exactly how you go about starting the buying or leasing process for yourself, what factors you need to consider, and how you actually go about making the deal.

Buying A Gas Station Business

A solidly profitable store may be sold with real estate and priced high compared to a mediocre store on a lease. It all depends on your personal finances. If you have a good bit of savings for a down payment along with good credit and other collateral, then you may be able to obtain a loan for a top-notch station that is profitable from the very first day.

Before you decide to go this route, there are few things you need to do to make sure you will be able to accomplish this goal.

Check your credit and make sure there are no errors or mistakes which are often found in 60% of credit reports.

Talk to a CPA. Have a personal financial statement prepared for you showing where your debt to income ratio is favorable after making the investment you're exploring.

Do an online appraisal of your home at a site like https://www.zillow.com.

Check the market value of your home or land and any other real estate investments you may have to see what equity lies in them.

Once you have determined that you have enough down payment, equity, and a well-established credit report on your side, you can start your search to find that perfect gas station to buy and operate.

Once you are at this point, the next step would be to contact some brokers and commercial real estate agents and let them know you are in the market for a store.

Make it known that you are only looking for stores with a proven financial track record and with real estate.

Once you get a list of all the available stores for sale, the most important part of this process will begin - determining which one to buy. This is by far the most important factor of the entire decision-making process. Once you can pick the winner, everything else will fall in the right place from that point on.

Gather a list of a few stores to consider; ask for as much information as they can provide to you. You may have to sign an NDA to be able to access the financials, but you can save some time by offering to do that early on.

Get professional help reviewing financials. Most times, a typical seller will provide 6-12 months of P&L or income statements.

Keep in mind that these financials are a good starting point to narrow down the choices, but they are only as good as the owner's word. The owner was responsible for providing sales and expense data to their accountant, so in other words, these are never the ultimate decider as these number can easily be manipulated to make it look more attractive than it actually is.

Assume now that you have narrowed your choices down to three stores after doing the basic review of the financials. Next, you need to physically visit the stores to get a feel of the business, look at the location in the neighborhood, and take plenty of notes.

One general rule of thumb is not to make it obvious or known to the cashier or person behind the counter that you are assessing the business to buy. Instead, keep it low profile and act like any other customer would do. You may have to visit each store more than once at a different time of the day to see different traffic flow so you can determine what prime business hours for that specific location are.

Once you have visited the stores and taken plenty of notes, it is time to create a worksheet like the one below. Draw a box where one side says "good," another side "not so good" or "bad" and the bottom will have a list of questions for the seller.

	GOOD	BAD
LOCATION		
TRAFFIC COUNT		
LAYOUT		

If you have more good than bad, it may be time for you to ask the agent to make a face-to-face meeting with the seller.

This grid is somewhat self-explanatory. Just remember, when you are looking at a business, you have to scrutinize it from many different angles, even from the angle of a customer and ask yourself these questions:

- Does this location have an easy in and out access?

- Does this location have too many competitors within a 1-2-mile radius?

- Does this location have enough parking compared to its nearest competitor?

- Does this location have any other advantages over its competitors?

- Does this location have any disadvantage compared to its competitors?

Once you answer these questions, you can then pick out where this location will go on the following MA/CP grid. By placing each business on the grid, you will see it becomes easy to make a decision on which one is the winner out of the few you are looking at.

	Market Attractiveness		
Competitive Strength	High	Medium	Low
High			
Medium			
Low			

If you can place any of the locations at the top left box of this grid, you have a sure winner, as both market attractiveness and competitive positioning of that location both are high, which is a true winner.

Leasing A Gas Station Business

Here's a scenario in which leasing might be better: if you only have $50,000 to $100,000 and average credit. If you find that your purchasing options are more limited, you probably have many more options leasing versus buying.

In this situation, you may still be able to find a station to buy with real estate. Try to find a station where the owner will agree to sell it to you on a vendor's lien. A vendor's lien refers to the right of a seller to repossess the property sold until the buyer makes all of the payments.

Often these types of stations are barely breaking even and require a more hands-on approach to make them profitable through excellent customer service to lower prices to be the most competitive store around and a top-notch marketing effort.

Contact some brokers and check the previously mentioned sites online to see what stores are available for lease. Conduct your research and consult a lawyer to see if you are ready to sign on the dotted line.

As I have mentioned, buying your gas station is likely the best option, but you have to do due diligence either way. Assuming you make the business a success, too, you can pretty much guarantee you are going to have more options and more flexibility down the road.

Below we talk about the politics of developing commercial sites, considering the fine print of business property contracts.

The Politics of Developing Commercial Real Estate Sites – The Fine Print for Any Business Owner Buying their Business Property

If you are buying land to build a gas station upon or if you are buying an existing gas station and want to remodel or rebuild parts of it, remember that the final determination for your investment is going to be identified based on whether or not you can obtain final and definitive approval for your plans for a given property. You need to secure approval for the use that you want to set the building for. Most of the time, the process for obtaining approvals involves three stages. All of the stages tend to be quite heavily affected by politics.

You are going to have to deal with the politics of your local council. This involves establishing who handles the community administration in terms of development and doing what you can to persuade them that your plans for usage in a given property are viable.

Becoming a real estate insider is going to be very important. Nothing is going to happen in a real estate market without advanced warning. Values for properties rarely change overnight, although they often appear to since most people are unaware of how to recognize the advanced warning signs of a coming change.

Even when properties are affected by a natural disaster, there is a fairly predictable pattern that you can observe and respond to. A person in the know will be acutely aware of these patterns and will be prepared to respond to them appropriately.

In downtown Manhattan, for example, there was a major drop in the value of real estate following 9/11. However, acute observers noted that the subsequent investment of major funds into the redevelopment of the area, plus the plans to rebuild and remodel the sites of the former World Trade Center towers were going to cause a major boom in the market. At present, the price of real estate downtown is skyrocketing.

Upward and downward movement, however, tends to come from new infrastructure (e.g., the Freedom Towers downtown), or from government action, such as investment efforts targeting a specific neighborhood. A real estate guru will study these types of developments very closely. The secret to your own success is going to depend on how well you can do this.

For one thing, you need to know that local government has control over real estate. Elected officials make up local government, and it is these elected officials, those who hold key roles in city functions, that you will need to defer to at some point if you need assistance securing permits.

Boards meet regularly to discuss decisions about real estate in the area and make judgments about all kinds of issues. Board members usually don't receive payment for their role, but they are generally assisted by volunteers. Every board or commission has a leader, a chairman, a commissioner, or a mayor. There may also be a handful of lawyers or paralegals involved in the management of city planning and zoning departments. The bottom line is that you are going to need to become an ally with these individuals.

The board of adjustment meets to discuss issues such as requests for modifications to or relief from certain ordinances imposed by the city or county. These issues are heard by the Board, which then makes a ruling.

The planning and zoning board provides considerable insight into the direction that communities are taking. For one thing, the planning and zoning board meets to discuss issues such as plans to develop new neighborhoods or redesign old ones. The board ultimately makes decisions relating to the future value of a property.

When you want to obtain approval for building plans, you are going to need to approach this particular community organization. First of all, you are going to have to review zoning rules. The next step is to hire a team that includes an architect, a civil engineer, a traffic consultant, and at least one reliable and experienced real estate lawyer. This team will help you deal with any zoning issues.

You are going to have to approach a development review committee or DRC. This group will include city or county building department heads, such as the fire marshal. The first meeting of the DRC is going to be an informal one. It is sometimes referred to as a pre-DRC meeting. Your design team will discuss what they want to do with the council members.

Following the preliminary DRC, you are going to have to schedule a formal DRC. At the formal hearing, the design team will discuss with the board what changes they should make to meet the requirements established by the DRC. A formal presentation will be made, and the DRC will then discuss any issues they still have with the plans.

Your design team will make their case, generally, lead by your real estate lawyer. The DRC will then vote to determine whether or not your plans are going to be allowed.

The best way to ensure that you don't have too many run-ins with the local authorities is to get to know a few real estate moguls in your area. You should strive to network with people who have successfully changed real estate values and who are likely to be able to help you change values for your own properties. You must build insider contacts for your local community and local authorities.

You should certainly familiarize yourself with all local zoning codes, and you should make it a regular practice to inspect "for sale" properties.

Another part of your routine is going to be focused on following the rental market for your area since rental prices will generally tell you what is going on in your investment area.

Finally, by learning the basics of income and expense statements plus studying whatever areas you are particularly weak in, you are positioning yourself to understand truly how to make sound investment decisions and how you are going to make a profit from your gas station business as part and parcel of a real estate investment.

Chapter 4: Due Diligence

The definition of due diligence is "reasonable steps taken by a person to satisfy a legal requirement, especially in buying or selling something. A comprehensive appraisal of a business undertaken by a prospective buyer, especially to establish its assets and liabilities and evaluate its commercial potential."

The key point in deciding which store or location to buy boils down to one point and one point only. The very important, century-old question that all prospective business owners have asked for hundreds of years, "Does this one make money?"

Send out a letter of intent, the details of which we will review in a later chapter. You have a formal agreement in the works between yourself and the seller of a property. It is your job, before you sign on any dotted line, to undertake some very important due diligence.

According to most expert real estate investors, you are going to need to complete the following steps before you accept a sale:

1. Assume nothing about the property – particularly about its value – until the seller has confirmed the information with valid documentation.

2. Hire a qualified building and land inspector to make an independent assessment of the property or properties that you are interested in.

3. Secure an inventory list from the seller and be sure to go through the building and double-check that all of the items listed are in fact in place.

4. Review all contracts presented to you by the seller or any other party involved in the deal. Be sure that you review the contracts at least once in the presence of your lawyer.

5. Initiate a certified property survey or request to receive a copy of a recently certified property survey.

6. With the help of your lawyer and real estate broker – or any other contact you deem appropriate – verify that the title for the property in question is valid.

7. Verify all liens and debts pertinent to the property.

8. Establish a timetable and checklist to ensure that you and your team have gone through all of the appropriate steps to make certain that the deal you enter into is going to be valid and that you are not going to be hit by any surprises.

On the business side, these are the following items you need to check or have someone qualified check on your behalf:

1. Last 2 years of books, including the monthly Profit and Loss (P&L) statement and the yearly balance sheet.

2. Sales tax records for the same period.

3. Hire a petroleum equipment company to check all of the petroleum and POS (Point of Sale) equipment and their current status.

4. Ask to see the tank registration for the current year.

5. Ask to see the existing fuel supply agreement and find out if you have to assume that agreement.

6. Ask to see the branding agreement. This is the agreement between the dealer and the oil companies like Shell, Exxon, and such.

7. Go visit the jobber who supplies the fuel to your station and try to negotiate a new fuel supply agreement that is more favorable to you.

8. Try to renegotiate a new 10-year branding agreement as most oil companies renew their branding

agreement every 10 years. They do offer a good sum of money for you to carry their brand upfront.

9. Ask the seller if there are any existing contracts for anything in the store that you have to assume and honor, such as payphone, vacuum, an air machine, or a deli brand food that they carry.

10. Always remember to read the fine print when it comes to these types of agreements.

Don't worry about appearing cynical; yes, it is cynical to take nothing at face value and to require your seller provide proof of everything they claim about their property, but it is also common sense.

Whether you are buying a house to live in or a gas station to be the base of your business, that doesn't change the reality that most sellers want to offload their properties and they think that the best way to do so is simply to avoid mentioning any problems associated with it.

The safest option for you is to ask if the seller can provide you with inspection reports and recent surveys at the beginning of the negotiations because you don't want to waste too much time pursuing a deal that, at the end of the day, can't go anywhere because of an insurmountable problem with the property.

Not to mention, you may well be contemplating a sizeable investment. There really is no advantage to rushing things when this type of money is involved.

Inspecting the Site

Hiring qualified inspectors are going to be a very significant step when it comes to getting independent verification of the status of a given property. For one thing, this might not be a straightforward proposition.

Good inspectors are not necessarily easy to find, but if you manage to get in touch with a few inspection companies, you should be able to compile a viable shortlist of professionals who may be able to help you.

To find a qualified inspector, as opposed, shall we say, to an inexperienced or inadequate one, you should look at their references and contact a couple of past clients to see how those projects have turned out. If possible, go back several years to determine whether any past clients have experienced any problems that their inspector should have been able to predict.

Next, you need to review a complete inventory list of the property holdings. You really cannot accept an inventory list at face value, either. You or someone you trust is going to have to go through the entire property and ensure that everything on the inventory list is where it should be and that it is in good condition.

In addition to a visual inspection of the property with a mind to verify the inventory, it is also a good idea to video record the check to ensure that you have evidence of your survey readily available.

The proper procedure for video recording preparation involves first indicating the date and time that the review is being conducted. If you have third parties involved in the inspection, you should introduce them at the beginning of the recording and confirm their role in the inspection. Note that at least one person taking part in the inspection will be from the seller's team.

To keep track of each area of the property that you are filming on the video, ensure that the room or location is announced as you enter or approach it. Providing a verbal introduction of this kind will help you keep track of any problems and will also provide further verification of any problems that you encounter.

The last thing you want to get involved in is a dispute about where there is an item missing or in less than good condition. If any item is missing or in need of repair, be sure to show it clearly and state the problem.

Remember that the work you put into verifying the details of the inventory of the prospective investment property is going to potentially save you thousands of dollars. For many major inventory lists, it is common for a considerable amount of money to slip through the cracks simply because the buyer is unaware of the need or is otherwise unwilling to conduct a thorough review of the inventory.

As I mentioned in the previous 10-point checklist about contracts, you are going to want to see everything relating to leased goods and fixtures in the building.

You will also need information on:

- Repair contracts

- Employment contracts

- Service contracts

- Insurance agreements and contracts

- Information on legal representation pertinent to the building

- Obligations established to municipal bonds

- Any other specific legal documents

You, as the buyer, may well become responsible for these agreements and contracts. You need to know as much as you can about what you are getting into, and if you disagree with any of the provisions detailed in any of these documents, you must contest them within a reasonable period before confirming the sale.

Before confirming the sale, you can communicate with the seller about the specific issues you have and, with luck, secure a remedy to the problem. There is nothing you can do to get out of any of these obligations once you have closed on the deal.

You are also going to need to obtain a certified property survey for your investment. Either you may request a copy of one that is already on file if it is relatively recent, or you may have to request one.

A viable survey of the property in question is going to include the legal address of the property, including the lot, block, subdivision, and bounds relating to the location. The street address should also be provided.

All of the property dimensions should be listed, including information about the exact location of any buildings and the specifics of their outside dimensions. All easements, including utility easements, must be noted as well, and any recent deed restrictions should be recorded on the survey.

The major problem with most property surveys, at least from the perspective of the inexperienced buyer, is that they are rarely compared to the actual property. You must make sure that the survey you are reviewing – that your lawyer reviews and that the title companies and banks review – is an accurate representation of the property and that any problems are accurately identified.

The lesson to be learned in due diligence is that you must either secure the assistance of a surveyor you can trust, or you must go yourself to verify that the survey of the property is, in fact, correct.

Finally, you are going to have to ensure that all titles and liens relating to the property are correct.

Ascertaining the validity of documents may seem like a lot of work, and you may be wondering whether it is necessary. After all, aren't legal documents the be-all and end-all? Don't they have to be accurate? Can't we trust lawyers? The simple and least cynical answer is that not every document is correct no matter how official it may look and no matter how many times it has been checked over.

When you are buying a property, the timetable for due diligence is often referred to directly in any formal contract that you are negotiating with your seller. For the most part, you will have between forty-five and sixty days to conduct your due diligence, although you may ask for extensions if there is some potential discrepancy that needs further examination.

With gas stations, the key things to watch for, as we will keep reiterating throughout this book, come down to access. And by access, I mean not only the actual physical access to the station but also access – the station's access – to customers and to a community of buyers.

Thinking outside of the box on what exactly this word, 'access' can mean, you'll quickly realize we're talking about the layout of the facility. Is it easy to navigate? Does it look good from the outside? Does it look inviting? Does it look clean? Does it look safe?

You'd be amazed how little people actually consciously think about these details until there's an indication that it's not inviting, nor is it clean.

By far, the most successful gas stations are the ones that are well maintained. The buildings are taken care of both in the sense that they are structurally sound and well maintained (i.e., clean and painted).

They are also well laid out. People don't feel like they are cramped or being spread too thin over a giant empty lot.

Stations should also be easy to spot and well lit, particularly at night. In fact, you might want to swing by your prospective properties to get a sense of how easy they are to find at night, in the dark. Does it look safe at night? What are the security features of the building, including the teller's booth?

You need to go with your instincts on some of this, as much as anything else. The more gas station properties you visit, too, the easier it should be to gauge the value of the property along these lines.

The last thing you are going to look into is a formal inspection of your property before you sign on the dotted line to become the owner. First of all, you are going to need to determine what to inspect; then you are going to need to assemble a qualified team of professionals whose opinions you trust.

You are then going to want to review all of the aspects that you have highlighted as being particularly significant. Once the survey is conducted, you are going to need to request a formal and comprehensive debriefing from your team relating to the details of the inspection and their findings.

For the most part, you are going to be surveying all critical elements of the property and, if there is an existing gas station business that you are taking over, you will review the details of that, too.

You should assess the property and the business details, as applicable, with your plans in mind, including any details on planned expansions of the station site.

If your inspectors deem that the property is inappropriate for your plans, then nothing else about the property matters. You must be able to use your property for your intended purpose. If you can't, then there is no point investing in it. You will simply end up owning a property that doesn't serve your purpose. Keep in mind those gas stations sites are going to be subject to certain requirements, including safety requirements.

Your inspectors should be able to tell you how well your plans fit the property and what cost elements you are going to have to address to implement your plans successfully. You may want to be working with someone who has experience inspecting gas station properties and businesses because of this; these details should be the principal focus of the inspection and these are the principle issues that you are going to be discussing with your inspection team.

Ideally, you should select an inspection team that understands your needs, not only the general aspects of real estate. For the most part, your team will include a property and building inspector and representatives from a title insurance company and your own lawyers.

It's crucial that whoever ends up on your inspection team, that you are aware both of their strengths and limitations. If there are limits to what each of the members will inspect and some crucial element or detail about the building is left uninspected, don't hesitate to take the time to find another inspector to fill in the missing details for you.

Unfortunately, inspections are one of the most underrated aspects of the whole process for investing in real estate. We've already mentioned that there tend to be problems with property surveys and that these often go unchecked. It is just as easy for you to miss a crucial detail about a property if you don't have an inspection team that is working together or at least able to coordinate their work in some meaningful way.

The best way to find an inspector is to check out the National Property Inspectors website at www.npiweb.com. This is by far your best bet to find a reputable, local contractor for a commercial inspection.

When you have your final consultation with your team of inspectors, ensure that you take the time to understand everything that they say. Make certain that you ask about the consequences of any potential problems or any actual problems that they have identified.

You should also be sure to ask them if there is anything, based on their assessment of everyone else's reports, that they want to re-examine or anything in their report that they would change in light of the other report findings.

Based on all of your work to review your prospective gas station properties, you can determine whether or not to go forward or stop the deal. The good news is that once you have obtained all of this information, you can be fairly sure of making the right investment decision - whether or not you should go ahead with the investment or put on the breaks.

Property Assessment Strategies

The commercial property market is made up of literally thousands of parcels of land and buildings. There are millions of individual properties with distinct attributes. The key to determining the difference between them and their respective values is the old adage of "location, location, location."

Now, you don't have to learn everything there is to know about commercial real estate to be successful in the gas station business, but it certainly helps to know something about property values and what to look for in a neighborhood as far as value goes.

Especially when you are buying a gas station business in the United States, you should make use of the information that is readily available to you and research some of it that is not.

The good news about property assessments, when you are looking to determine whether or not you can obtain a profit, is that you can identify factors that affect the values of real estate quite easily. It is important to understand how each of the factors moves the value of a property up or down.

The key to success in the assessment of real estate value is basically that you need to use your knowledge of real estate to ascertain what you can do with each property to determine what to buy and how you can maximize each property to make a viable profit on your sale.

You are also going to have to be quite shrewd about how you assess the impact of each factor, noting that some factors can cause one property to go up in value while at the same time, the same factors can cause another similar property to go down in value. Two properties could be virtually identical and still have an entirely different approach to value.

The first thing that you are going to want to assess about each property you consider is the access. Access is a means of entering or leaving a property and something many inexperienced buyers take for granted. Two properties that are very similar and even positioned across from each other on an intersection to have a quite different degree of accessibility. Look at the access to each property you are interested in to determine whether it is viable for both pedestrians and vehicular traffic.

The greater the access to a property, the higher the value of the property based on this factor, however, you are going to need to determine that the legal elements are in place to allow for access via the various different roadways or via the frontage. Difficult access renders any property valueless to a user since virtually every business and residential client is going to need to have good access to their respective properties.

Contact the department of transportation for your city or county to confirm what permits are in place and what the details for access are for each property you review. This is part of the due diligence process we have talked about.

If there is a problem with access, determine what you can do to improve access to the site, if anything. If the site has existing access, verify that it is a legal entrance and exit for the use of the property. Many existing businesses have time codes or establish regulations via the DOT that allow maneuvers such as curb cuts, turn lanes, and entrance and exit driveways for limited periods. Check all of this.

The next thing you are going to want to consider with each property is the demographics of the community.

The demographic data is going to tell you about the physical and economic nature of the community. You are going to know the number of the families in the area, and you are going to have to know what the various concentrations of populations are within the community.

Demographic makeup always plays a very important role in determining what kind of value a building can have within a specific location. For example, an apartment building designed to house families – that is, a building with a considerable number of two and three-bedroom apartments – is probably going to do quite well in a community that is particularly popular with families based on, for example, the proximity of quality schools.

Since you will have done your research to become familiar with the areas in which you're operating, discovering demographic information is going to be relatively straightforward.

The more you get to know your community, the more likely it is that you will be able to determine accurately whether or not the demographics of the community is going to increase or decrease the value of your business.

If you drive around and visit several gas stations in your area, you're bound to find that they do a whole variety of different things on the side. For instance, some gas stations may have a mini restaurant (Deli) with a separate seating area for people to sit and enjoy a quick bite to eat. If it is appropriate for the market, you are going to want to consider it, too.

A third factor you are going to have to look into to determine the profitability of your target location is the traffic count.

Traffic counts are conducted by local authorities and available to the public via the city or county department of transportation. At the very least, they are going to be able to direct you to where you can get your hands on a copy of the reports.

If possible, you should try to obtain older reports for the same area. The idea is that you need to identify trends for traffic reports, putting as much information as you can get into context.

At the end of the day, when it comes to traffic counts, you need to make sure that you pay attention to the long-term plans for all department of transportation changes. Roadway alterations have long planning stages, so you should look out for plans that are likely to change the traffic flow past a building, limit it, or otherwise increase it one way or another.

Keep in mind that sometimes too much traffic can affect a gas station business adversely, it is often true when an intersection is really busy, consumers tend to avoid stopping in or around that intersection because of the fear of getting back into that heavy traffic again. So, the lesson is too much of good thing can sometimes be bad also.

The last thing you want to do is open up a gas station on a street that is about to be by-passed by a redesigned highway or something. This situation is relatively rare. You would be very unlucky to have this happen to you, but then again, bad luck follows those who don't do their homework. Find out as much as you can about what is coming to a neighborhood that you are considering for your gas station business.

In terms of traffic flow, you are going to need to observe which way the traffic generally goes and at what times of the day. A study of the roadways, however cursory, should help you make this determination. Find out also if there are alternate routes that draw traffic away from the property you are reviewing and think about the effect that this might have upon the overall value of your building.

Remember that traffic flow is very significant to property value both in terms of determining the physical accessibility of a site and the visual access for the property. You need to weigh up both of these factors to determine whether, all in all, you have a property that is both easy to see and easy to access.

You are going to combine your findings relating to access, the traffic flow, and count, and the demographics of the community to determine whether or not the building you're reviewing is worth investing in and whether or not it will serve your specific needs.

So far, I've covered the primary factors that determine the value of a property. However, there are a few other elements you are going to want to consider.

Look at the school district into which the property falls. In fact, because these are going to be among your top customers, you are going to want to know as much as you can about the type of people that go to the school, the parents and the children. If you determine that there are lots of young families in the area – couples with young kids, both parents working –selling certain kinds of goods in your store is likely to prove an extremely viable business.

For instance, if you have a lot of school kids in the area of your gas station, you are going to get after-school business simply by selling the kinds of food and drink kids like to buy after school. How about offering a pick-and-mix candy area? What about potato chips, ice cream, or even pizza?

You're also going to need to find out about plats. These are documents that contain information about approached and recorded drawings for tracts of land. These may detail an entire subdivision or just a small parcel of land.

The idea is that you can use these documents as part of your assessment to figure out the value of a property, observing the rules and regulations of city, county, or state in which the land in question is located.

A plat includes the following information about properties/land areas:

- The legal description of each site from the point of time that the plat was approved by the local governing body.

- Property dimensions for each property featured within a plat.

- Plat items including information on roadways, easements for roads and utilities, and any other elements such as ponds or canals that have a defining influence upon the site.

- Plat notes that detail what approved bodies have been added to the plat and any details about the site that are considered important, such as restrictions and any pertinent information about zoning or building codes.

- The date of the plat will also be included in the document as well as information about the various uses of the plat over time.

The deciding factor for any investment is the use of the building. Use governs the value of a property. All of the factors detailed in this chapter can increase or decrease the value of a property. They will need to be reviewed in terms of whether or not the property is useful and whether or not it can be used for many elements.

Now, as your goal is to set up a gas station business, you can approach any property you look at intending to establish the usage for this commercial venture. Usage can be achieved by virtually anyone as all it requires is a basic understanding of what the various authorities want in terms of property use and what you can do to match their wants, detailed by their regulations, with a void in the community.

The bottom line with use is whether you are buying a gas station business that is already running or you are setting one up essentially from scratch, don't make too many assumptions about the property you are buying as your base. Make sure you determine first what the zoning regulations are and whether or not the zoning regulations can be changed.

Any purchase agreement you negotiate with a seller should allow you time to determine whether or not you can obtain approvals to rezone a property if that is what you require for your business purposes. The key to investment success is always going to be starting off within the zoning regulations for a given building and then securing the applications for rezoning if that fits in with your objectives.

Assessing the Business Aspect

To assess the functioning of your prospective gas station purchase as an actual business (and you are going to do this in part, too, based on a review of the exterior), ask to see all the invoices the store received from vendors in one given month, you can ask this when you ask for the other items I mentioned in due diligence earlier.

Once you receive these invoices, add up the value of what the vendors are bringing in and organize them by category. Look at the sales report for that same month and add up the sales.

Through a basic comparison of purchases from vendors and sales, you should have a pretty good idea of where the money is actually being made (if it is actually being made) at a given store.

Assuming you are looking at a few stations, that you have at least two or three sites on a shortlist, you now at least know which store makes the most money out of all.

While this is an important factor, assessing the business value of a gas station, it is not the only factor. We still need to see what the expenses of those stores are to determine which store makes the most net profit, also known as the "take-home money."

One important factor to ask the seller is the status of their UST (Underground Storage Tanks) and if they are in compliance with your state environmental requirements. I will cover more about UST later in this book, as this is an extremely vital part of your business.

Finally, you now know which pick on your list nets the most money, but also consider a few issues, like the distance to and from your home, the safety of the neighborhood, and the overall attractiveness of the location.

Even if a gas station is not making a fortune right now, even if the take-home is only moderate, looking at all of the information you should now have. It may be clear to you already what you can do to enhance the business and increase profitability. We are also going to discuss some of the better strategies for increasing profit in Part II of this book.

Measure up the various pros and cons for your top choices and consider how prepared you are to put up with the cons in the long-term.

When you have an idea of the scenario that looks best to you, you have your gas station choice, and you need to get ready to go forward and sign that purchase agreement.

Chapter 5: Financing

There are a few ways to finance your purchase. You can always stop in and talk to your local bank that you already bank with to see what their requirements are. You can also contact a local reputable mortgage broker who can find other non-local lenders who specialize in deals such as yours.

You can go to the website for the Small Business Association (SBA) for some information and see which one of their loans you qualify for as they have various loan programs to fit most needs.

The SBA is the official organization in the United States that works to support the interests of small businesses around the country. As you may already know, small businesses, including the kind of gas station business you are considering, make up an important backbone for the United States economy.

Addressing just some of the many challenges that small businesses face, the SBA provides a variety of loans and other support, including free advice from experienced business professionals (often very well worth it).

The SBA can also help you get a handle on the type of loans you may be eligible for as you start to build your gas station business.

It is always a good idea to apply at more than one lender. Once you gather a few loan applications, it is time to prepare some documents for your loan package.

A typical commercial loan package should include the followings:

- A detailed business plan, like the one included in the back of this book

- Your updated resume highlighting the relevant business experience

- A recent signed personal financial statement, preferably one that has been prepared by a CPA

- Copies of the last 3 years of personal tax returns

- A copy of the purchase agreement that you signed with the seller

- A current P&L of the business

- A projected P&L of the business

Most commercial lenders will also ask for some environmental testing reports like Phase I and or Phase II testing of the premises.

It can typically take anywhere from 30 to 90 days from application submission to actually closing on the loan, especially if the SBA is involved. Generally, the SBA requires more documentation than other banks.

One point to note, when you sign a purchase agreement and put earnest money towards a deposit, make sure there is a clause in that agreement that clearly states that you will only buy the location if you can get "favorable financing from a lender." These words can also act as an exit strategy in case you want to back out at some point in this process. This way, you will also get back all of your deposit.

Financing Analysis Pointers for Commercial Property Purchases

In most cases, the financing is underwritten based on the merits of the individual case. That is, no hard and fast rule determines whether you can get a loan for a commercial property.

You can probably apply the same principle when you're working with a team of partners to secure your investment. Anyone you work with on your investment deal is going to have their own unique set of criteria and their own process of evaluating the merits of the deal you're proposing. Acknowledging this is the first step to getting around it as a potential problem.

As we said before, gas stations are particularly good on the numbers. They are generally an easy business to run, and gas is one of those products, right now, that pretty much everyone needs. Plus, you can upsell with a whole variety of other items in the store.

The key to understanding how you're going to get the financing you need is to find a straightforward but meaningful way to break down the most important numbers used in analyzing potential loans. The first step to doing this involves looking at the various critical factors that almost every lender uses when analyzing a potential loan.

The first thing to consider is the "processing" of a loan. This refers to the attempt made by lenders to verify the numbers associated with a purchase or refinancing of the property. Processing is basic due diligence for any lender. The findings should demonstrate beyond a reasonable doubt that neither the buyer nor the owner of the given property will be overburdened by debt as a result of buying or refinancing the property in question.

Potential lenders are going to verify this by looking at both the property and the principle buyer to assess the strengths and potential weaknesses of each case, however, there are some general aspects of the analysis that you can predict and research yourself.

Commercial mortgage lending ratios are frequently used as a means of determining whether or not buyers can handle the transactions. Your potential investors and anyone contemplating offering you a loan on your property investment are going to consider the various ratios described below:

1. Loan To Value Ratio (LTV)

The Loan to Value Ratio (LTV) is defined as follows:

Loan to Value = Total loan balances (1st mortgage + 2nd mortgage) ÷ Fair market value (as determined by a third party appraisal)

The loan to value ratios on commercial mortgages seldom exceeds 75%. This means that the lender funds no more than 75% of the fair market value. This can sometimes leave the buyer short, requiring the buyer to put down a larger down payment. Coast investors and other specialty lenders lend up to 90% on owner-occupied real estate.

2. Debt Service Coverage Ratio (DSCR)

Debt Service Coverage Ratio (DSCR) evaluates the ratio of property income to property debt. The debt service coverage ratio is defined as:

Debt Service Coverage Ratio = Net Operating Income ÷ Debt Service

Debt service is the mortgage payment on the property. Most lenders insist that the DSCR ratio exceed 1.15. A debt service coverage ratio of less than 1.0 generally means that the property did not produce enough net rental income for the owner to make the mortgage payments without supplementing the property from their personal budget.

3. Personal Debt Service Coverage Ratio

Some lenders of small commercial loans (less than $1,000,000) also look at the personal income and debt of the borrowers. If you develop a partnership agreement, this type of review will generally involve lenders looking closely at your debt situation and the situation of your partners as well.

The personal debt ratio compares the dollar amount of the bills that a borrower must pay each month to the amount of monthly income he earns from all sources. More precisely, the personal debt coverage ratio is defined as:

Personal Debt Coverage Ratio = Monthly Personal Debt ÷ Monthly Personal Income

A personal debt ratio of 150% means that a borrower's obligations are one and a half times his income. Obviously, someone whose personal debt coverage ratio is 150% is in trouble. Personal debt ratios seldom are allowed to exceed 50% in practice.

Several other important calculations used in assessments by lenders are described below. When you are making your own assessment of a property value and the viability of a deal with your partners, you should certainly consider these elements as a means of reviewing how the numbers are going to play out in your investment.

- Net Operating Income (NOI): this is the income from a rental property after deducting for real estate taxes, fire and liability insurance, maintenance, and all other operating expenses.

- Capitalization Rate (Cap Rate): this is a ratio used to estimate the value of income-producing properties. In general, the lower the cap rate, the higher the selling price of the property will be.

For your own purposes, you need to analyze two key financial factors in addition to the factors mentioned above as a means of ensuring the overall validity of your overall investment decision.

Your first consideration in this respect is going to be the property analysis or, more specifically, the property's fair market value. Fair market value is determined by the appraisal and by fair market rents (the average rent paid in your market for properties similar to yours).

Age, appearance, local market, location, and accessibility are some other factors to consider when analyzing the property.

NOI, DSCR, LTV, and the Cap Rate

I know these acronyms above look very foreign, but they are important finance terms when it comes to financing a business. I will explain what they are and how to calculate them below. The steps for obtaining, calculating, and interpreting the four most critical numbers about any loan amount you receive are discussed in this chapter.

As in the previous chapters, the basis of this section is the provision of a review of the key numbers that play a role in the loan process.

Net Operating Income (NOI)

This number plays an important role early on in the loan process. Subtracting vacancies and operating expenses from a property's gross income determine NOI.

Operating expenses include the following items:

- Advertising

- Insurance

- Maintenance

- Property taxes

- Property management

- Repairs

- Supplies

- Utilities

The more information you include to undertake this calculation, the more accurate your results will be.

While more information is better when figuring the NOI, be sure not to include anything which is not an operating expense. Operating expenses *do not include:*

- Improvements such as a new roof

- Personal property like a lawnmower

- Mortgage payments

- Income taxes

- Capital gains taxes

- Loan origination fees

Debt Service Coverage Ratio (DSCR)

A key component in making an underwriting evaluation of a commercial property is the debt service coverage ratio - defined as the yearly debt payment compared to the adjusted gross income of the property in question.

Debt Service Coverage Ratio = Net Operating Income ÷ Debt Service

By using a DSCR of 1:1.15, a lender is saying that they are looking for a $1.15 in net income for each $1.00 mortgage payment.

Typically a lender will determine the DSCR ratio based on annual figures and comparing the yearly mortgage payment to the yearly net borrower income.

The higher the DSCR ratio is, the more conservative the lender will be. Most lenders will never go below a 1:1 ratio (a dollar of debt payment per dollar of income available). At a 1:1 ratio, a property is breaking even.

Anything less than a 1:1 ratio means the potential borrower is in a negative cash flow situation, thus raising the risk for the lender.

DSCR's depend on property type and what a lender perceives the risk to be. Today, lenders consider apartment properties the least risky category of investment lending. With gas stations, the perceived risk can vary dramatically. Lenders are more inclined to use smaller DSCR's when evaluating a loan request, though, simply because they may not know the particulars of the gas station industry. Be ready with a contingency plan if the numbers are not quite what you wanted.

Loan to Value (LTV)

Unlike residential lending, lenders are more conservative with commercial investment properties. Many require a minimum of 35% of the purchase price. Some will loan up to 90% of the purchase price to buyers based upon a buyer's creditworthiness and property analysis, but this is rare.

The percentage of the purchase price which the lender is willing to loan is called the Loan to Value (LTV) percentage, defined as the calculation of the loan amount divided by the purchase price, expressed in a percentage format.

$$\text{Loan Amount} \div \text{Purchase Price} = \text{LTV \%}$$

Each lender is different and decides their LTV based upon the lender's enthusiasm for the project, the quality of the buyer, and the property.

Capitalization Rate (Cap Rate)

This is a ratio used to estimate the value of income-producing properties. Defined as the net operating income (NOI) of a commercial property, divided by the sales price or value of the property, and expressed as a percentage.

$$\text{NOI} \div \text{Purchase Price} = \text{Cap Rate \%}$$

Investors, lenders, and appraisers use the cap rate to estimate the purchase price for different types of income-producing properties. So if you have the cap rate and the Net operating income of a property, you can determine the property's true value or purchase price.

$$NOI \div Cap\ Rate\ \% = Purchase\ Price$$

A market cap rate is determined by evaluating the financial data of similar properties that have recently sold in a specific market. It provides a more reliable estimate of value than a market Gross Rent Multiplier (GRM) since the cap rate calculation utilizes more of a property's financial detail.

The GRM calculation only considers a property's selling price and gross rents. The cap rate calculation incorporates a property's selling price, gross rents, non-rental income, vacancy amount, and operating expenses. Thus, the cap rate provides the most reliable estimate of value.

When dealing with a seller and an interested buyer for a particular piece of income property, the seller is trying to get the highest price for the property. The lower the cap rate, the higher the price a seller will command. Thus, the buyer hopes for a higher cap rate to keep the selling price low.

Investors and lenders, as well as buyers, look for high cap rates. Remember, the lower the selling price, the higher the cap rate. The higher the selling price, the lower the cap rate. In summary, investors, lenders, and buyers prefer a higher cap rate.

The cap rate varies in different areas of the country and even in different areas of a city for many reasons such as the desirability of a location, level of crime, and the general condition of an area.

You would expect lower capitalization rates in newer or more desirable areas of a city and higher cap rates to compensate for the added risk in less desirable areas. In a real estate market where net operating incomes are increasing, and cap rates are declining over time for a given type of investment property, such as office buildings, property values are generally on the rise. If net operating incomes are decreasing and capitalization rates are increasing over time in a given marketplace, property values are declining.

During periods of increasing interest rates, the cap rates rise along with the interest rates. This cap rate increase results from a drop in property prices associated with the higher cost of money.

During periods of decreasing interest rates, such as the one experienced from the year 2000 to 2005, the cap rates decrease as interest rates come down. The net result is that property prices decrease, and properties become more affordable.

Be aware that the frequency of sales for commercial income properties in a given marketplace may be low. If so, reliable capitalization rate data may not be available. If you can obtain a market cap rate from an appraiser or lender for the type of property you are evaluating, check to see if the cap rate value was determined with recent sales of comparable properties or if it was constructed.

When adequate financial data is unavailable, appraisers may construct a cap rate through analysis of its component parts, thus reducing the credibility of the results. Cap rates determined by evaluating the recent actions of buyers and sellers in a particular marketplace will produce the best market value estimate for a property.

If you can obtain a market cap rate, you can then use this information to estimate what similar income properties should sell for. This will help you to gauge whether or not the asking price for a particular piece of property is high or low.

Review:

    Cap Rate = NOI / Value

And:

Estimated Value = NOI / Cap Rate

If a property has an NOI of $120,000 and you have determined that cap rates in the area for this type of property average 12%, then the formula is:

Market Value = 120,000 / 12%.

This gives you an estimated market value of $1,000,000. Remember, as the cap rate goes down, selling prices go up; therefore this same formula, calculated with a lower cap rate of 6% raises the price to $2,000,000. Conversely, a higher cap rate of 15% would give you an estimated property value of $800,000.

Types of Loans and Lenders

Many entrepreneurs are not fully aware of the increasing availability of small loans from bigger banks, conduit lenders, or agencies that have traditionally targeted larger loans. That means that some investors are likely to be paying higher rates and accepting more onerous terms than necessary.

The best loan for a given deal should reflect the borrower's financial goals. Consider your goals when discussing term length, leverage level, interest rate, speed and certainty of execution, reserve requirements, and any other pertinent factors. As you expect to hold on to your gas station property for the longer term, see if you can take advantage of the low-rate environment, and lock in fixed-rate deals at high leverage levels from lenders.

Commercial Loans Based on Credit

Loans secured by real estate can be divided into two categories based on the source of repayment: credit-based loans and project financing.

Credit-based loans are secured by real estate but are to be repaid from the borrower's business operations or personal assets. Although the primary collateral for the loan is real estate, the real estate is not the source of repayment.

In many instances, these loans finance the acquisition of an owner-occupied business property that has an economic life similar to the term of the loan. They can also be term loans used for other business purposes, such as working capital. In either case, repayment expectation derives from the cash flow of the business rather than from the underlying real estate.

Purchasing or Re-Financing with a Hard Money Mortgage

Hard money comes through many channels. One of the most common ways is mortgages. Using the owner's equity in real estate, hard money lenders generally lend 65% to

70% of the value of the real estate property. Hard money mortgages generally support commercial purposes.

Lending criteria for hard money mortgages are straightforward. The loan depends on the value of the 'subject property.'

If the borrower is buying the subject property, the value of the real estate is defined as the actual purchase price of the property.

If the borrower already owns the subject property but needs hard money to refinance, the value depends on a written real estate appraisal.

To take advantage of ongoing projects, investors often require more operating capital than conventional banks are prepared to provide on short notice.

Hard money works best as a bridge loan to acquire the property and make improvements. Terms generally range from one to three years. This provides an ample period for the borrower to prepare the property and his personal financial status to arrange for long-term conventional financing. Alternatively, this one to three-year period allows the borrower to arrange for the sale of the property.

Another reason to seek a hard money loan is to prevent foreclosure on the property. Such loans are the specialty that brings out the best and the worst in hard money lenders.

Hard money lenders can fund a real estate purchase or refinance loan in as little as two weeks from the time all your documentation is in their hands. It is even possible to get it done in less time.

Documents to Provide to Hard Money Lenders

- Written real estate appraisal with photos

- Purchase contract (if you are purchasing the property)

- Personal financial statement

- Income statement for the borrower

- 3 yrs P&L for the property, if it is income-producing

- 3 yrs of tax returns for the borrower

- Statement of use of funds

- Proof of where the balance of funding will come from, such as a bank statement showing the funds available, if you are buying the property

Being prepared with a complete package will expedite your funding.

Bridge Loans

Typically, a bridge loan is a type of loan with a shorter term limit and may be the best financing tool for some difficult situations.

A bridge loan's terms range from just a few days to as long as five years. A great example of a bridge loan is a typical neighborhood blue-collar Pay Day Lender that lends money to individuals against their next paycheck.

In commercial real estate, bridge loans are used to enable a quick closing, allowing the borrower to take advantage of an opportunity and arrange for longer-term financing at his or her leisure.

Real estate bridge loans are used for both purchases and refinancing. Speed is often of paramount importance in bridge loans.

Investors in the income-producing commercial real estate are frequently required to manage certain challenges that impact net income, value, or both. Some investors see these challenges as problems while others see the same challenges as opportunities.

These problems or opportunities include the following:

- Incomplete financial reports

- Change of use

- Receivership

- Poor physical condition

- Debt buy-down opportunity

- Lack of adequate seasoning

- Debtor-in-possession

- Foreclosure

- Partnership Liquidation

- Chapter 11 Bankruptcy filing

An owner facing the above problems is probably also facing an immediate need to refinance due to a maturing loan. For a purchaser seeking below market values, the other investor's problems become his opportunity to make a below-market acquisition. In any of the above situations, a bridge loan may be the best, or, perhaps, the only option.

Put another way, a bridge loan is a short-term loan on a property that does not yet qualify for a conventional or permanent loan for various reasons. Generally, bridge loans are risky for the lender. The property is the primary collateral for the loan, but as a result of various problems, the property may not be financially stable.

Often, historical and current revenues will not support traditional lending criteria. The "hair" on the deal will range widely, meaning you, as the broker, will have to address a wide range of problems. The problems plaguing the loan may involve the property, the borrower, or the transaction itself. Often, the problems involve a combination of all three.

The Importance of Appraisals to Your Financing Options

Once you have a shortlist of properties for your gas station business, you will need to get an appraisal.

An appraisal, in its most basic terms, is a written opinion of real estate value as of a specific date. When prepared by a qualified appraiser, it represents an independent and impartial analysis of all the relevant data. Because market value is not apparent just from a visual inspection, an appraisal is usually required when a property is sold, taxed, insured, or financed.

Licensed appraisers must adhere to the Uniform Standards of Professional Appraisal Practice (USPAP), which became effective in 1993. These rules have established a high level of professional and ethical standards which all licensed appraisers must follow.

You may, of course, be somewhat familiar with residential appraisals if you are a homeowner. However, industry-standard forms are used for most residential appraisals while narrative reports are prepared for commercial properties.

All appraisal reports for commercial properties contain facts and analysis of the subject property, the neighborhood, and the market.

Standard records tend to include rent roll information (if applicable) as of the date of the appraisal, and income and expenses for the property for both year-to-date and previous year.

Commercial appraisals contain exhibits, including photographs of the subject and comparable properties, a detailed scale sketch of the subject, a map showing the subject in relation to the comparables, and a flood plan map showing the subject property. All appraisal reports contain a

Statement of Limiting Conditions and an Appraiser's Certification.

Appraisal of Market Value

The appraisal report includes information on the area economy, factors which influence neighborhood market value, characteristics of the site including any improvements, and identification or analysis of any other factors which might impact the value of the subject property.

These are three approaches I have seen to a good appraisal.

1. **COST APPROACH:** This approach is based on the proposition that the informed purchaser would pay no more than the cost of producing a substitute property with the same utility as the subject property. It is particularly applicable when the property being appraised involves relatively new improvements, which represent the highest and best use of the land or when unique or specialized improvements are located on the market.

    This method involves estimating the reproduction cost of the new improvements, then subtracting accrued depreciation from all sources. To this is added the market value of the land, which has been found by completing a direct sales comparison. In fast-growing areas with restricted land availability, the value of the land may surpass the value of the structure as area redevelopment takes place.

2. **DIRECT SALES COMPARISON:** This approach is based on the proposition that an informed purchaser would pay no more for a property than the cost of acquiring an existing property with the same utility.

    This approach is applicable when an active market provides sufficient quantities of reliable data, which can be verified. This involves comparing the subject property to actual sales of similar properties, with appropriate adjustments being made for any differences between the properties. Various unit values are developed which, when applied to like units of the subject, give an indication of value for the subject.

3. **INCOME APPROACH:** This is the procedure, which converts anticipated benefits (dollar income or amenities) derived from ownership of the property into a value estimate. This technique relates to the future benefits arising out of property ownership, such as current and anticipated future income. The benefits are estimated by deducting fixed and operating expenses from the gross potential annual income, to

arrive at the net operating income, which is required to attract capital to the property.

Factors to Consider Specific to Gas Stations

There is a lot of information to process, but the purchase of a gas station involves a number of legal factors that must be considered and discussed with your business lawyer before finalizing.

The key consideration for signing on the dotted line is whether the gas station you are buying is a "franchised" or "independent" operation.

Franchised gas stations operate according to a "franchise agreement" with a national supplier like Exxon or Sunoco.

Independent stations, on the other hand, do not have a national supplier. Rather, they sell "unbranded" fuel procured from an assortment of regional suppliers.

The key advantage of the franchised station is the instantaneous name recognition, trademarks, trade design, and canopies available and associated with the national brand.

If you consider this option, you need to review terms of the franchise agreement with an attorney and consider whether the franchisor will approve your purchase of the station. You also need to closely review the quotas or requirements for fuel sales related to the franchise agreement, the rebates that may or may not be paid to you for fuel sales, and issues, potential or actual, with the ownership and maintenance of fuel pumps and tanks.

You need to know, for instance, who owns the pumps and the tanks as these are the most critical assets affecting the daily operations and profitability of a franchised business.

Not every seller of a gas station owns the pumps and tanks. In fact, it is common for national franchisors or the property owner, if the gas station is located on leased property, to own these assets.

If you are evaluating the purchase of a particular gas station, you must determine:

- Exactly who owns the pumps and tanks

- Whether the sale includes the transfer of the pumps and tanks

- Whether the property is leased or on leased land

- What the terms of that lease are

- What, if any, is the repair history for the pumps and tanks. They must comply with all regulatory requirements.

As another check, you should verify the environmental history of the station you are looking at and assess any issues of prior contamination concerning the tanks. Evaluate the utilization of the environmental contingency clause in the purchase agreement and obtain a Phase I environmental site assessment to ensure that you are not biting off more than you can chew.

Chapter 6: Closing the Deal

Once you secured the loan, it's time to set up a date for the actual closing, but before doing so there are few key things to remember.

Inventory Valuation at Cost

Among other things, you need to ask for a meeting with the seller to discuss the date and how to handle the inventory count. Hire a reputable company that does inventory counting.

Remember every item in the store is priced at retail and you should only pay the wholesale or actual cost of that inventory and not retail price. Typically, it is decided between the buyer and seller a day or two before the actual closing.

It is always a good idea to ask the seller a week or 10 days in advance to shrink the inventory and keep the gasoline at a minimum and not to fill the tank, since gasoline prices are so volatile you never want to buy too much of it in advance.

Ask the seller if they have any prior inventory count sheet from a previous month so you can get an idea as to how much they have. It can serve as a benchmark for you.

The most common practice is to hire a company that you and the seller both agree on that specializes in inventory counting. Have them come the day of the closing. Once they finish the count, they usually furnish an itemized inventory report at retail cost. Then it is time for you and the seller to sit down and calculate the actual cost of that retail inventory, which you will owe to the seller as part of your closing costs.

In this industry, a typical closeout is usually done where fuel is paid at the last load cost, where merchandise is usually done around 25%-30% less the retail cost.

To simplify this, let's say the store inventory closeout report showed $80,000 in merchandise at retail, so the actual cost for this inventory will be (provided you and the seller decided at 28% of retail to be the actual cost):

80,000 X 0.28= $22,400

Now we deduct that from the total, which is:

$80,000-$22,400= $57600

This is your actual cost.

Wrapping Your Head Around the Closing

One of the most perplexing aspects of real estate deals for many people is closing. Just imagine what a tough time real estate brokers have. They get tons of calls every day from people who say they're interested in such as such property.

At the end of the day, when buying and selling real estate, the transfer of real estate ownership is rarely straightforward. First of all, we're talking about major financial transactions. Several hundred thousand dollars, as a respectable average, is a lot of money. A building or piece of land is also a very valuable commodity. Both the buyer and the seller in any real estate deal are looking to make out. They want a good deal; as the saying goes, "I can pay your price if you accept my terms."

Closing a deal is always about negotiation. The terms of any deal can be modified, and the price of any commodity can be adjusted. The basic idea is that you should be looking to promote a win-win situation for all parties, yourself included. The process of buying or selling properties should make use of a whole range and perhaps several different combinations of investment tools you have at your disposal.

A few years ago, I came to understand that there is no standard contract when it comes to commercial real estate, which was an expensive but very valuable lesson for me. Whether it is a lease, a purchasing agreement, or an operating agreement, most of a contract is subject to negation in commercial real estate.

It is exceptionally rare for any commercial real estate agreement to be accepted as it is first presented to the buyer and seller. The agreement, at the end of the day, is very comprehensive. It tends to be necessary to pay close attention to every item in a commercial leasing document.

Unfortunately, many lawyers have a habit of complicating contracts, filling them with legal jargon so obscure that few people can decipher it. Often, these complicated contracts are developed to protect clients from every possible problem and to anticipate every possible circumstance. Other contracts, the polar opposite, might be too general and may fail to define and delineate key points of an agreement. Of course, contracts that are too general are often not spotted until it is too late until there is a problem between the buyer/renter and the seller/tenant.

The best time to negotiate a contract to close a deal is at the beginning of the process. You do not want to head into any kind of legal battle without a contract that not only protects you but allows you some degree of flexibility.

To establish a contract that will close your deals effectively, you need the assistance of an experienced and qualified real estate lawyer. You have to make certain – with your lawyer's help – that any agreement you sign or otherwise commit to is fully comprehensible to you and that it represents your interests effectively. There's no point going into an agreement blind.

If any contigencies need to be renegotiated in your opinion, you should have them ironed out before you sign.

The Journey from Negotiation to Closing

So what happens when you are actually ready to buy or lease your gas station property? What tactics should you use to bring about the closing process as effectively and efficiently as possible?

The answers offered by many commercial real estate aficionados are that you should use a series of tactics to negotiate your deal. By the time you get through each of the steps in the series, you will have your deal, signed, sealed, and delivered.

The often-cited negotiation steps are as follows:

- Step 1: Present the buyer with a letter of intent

- Step 2: Suggest several options for the sale including:

    o Propose an options contract

    o Consider split funding

- - Suggest a seller-held mortgage
  - Offer a partial release
  - Offer a real estate exchange
- Step 3: Discuss all options with the seller
- Step 4: Decide on an option and consult your real estate attorney
- Step 5: Draft, negotiate, and then redraft a contract
- Step 6: Sign on the dotted line

Letter of Intent

First, a letter of intent is designed to ensure that a commercial real estate transaction – in this instance, the sale of a gas station or space suitable for use as a gas station – is as straightforward and time-efficient as possible from beginning to end. In many cases, letters of intent are used by real estate professionals as a means of expediting deals, cutting the amount of time and effort required to get from having an offer made on a property to having a legally executed contract ready to sign.

A letter of intent serves to outline what is considered a preliminary agreement or understanding between the buyer and seller. However, many parties there may be involved in a given transaction.

These letters are in no way going to bind you to anything. They don't serve as legal documents. Their purpose is to help you to start laying out important business terms that you will subsequently accept or reject in your legally binding contract. As we emphasize throughout this book, conducting due diligence when it comes to business is essential. Writing a letter of intent is a key tool in due diligence.

Topics to cover in your standard letter of intent include the following:

- Timing of the agreement

- The monetary terms

- Details of the financing

- Any deal contingencies

- The specifics of risk allocation

- Details of any forms of documentation to be used

- Specifics about who will prepare the documentation for the formal agreement

A well-drafted letter of intent that covers all of the necessary points provides something of a safety net for you, and the other parties involved in the deal. For one thing, it helps to avoid misunderstandings. It also serves to bind you and the other parties to the deal, both psychologically and morally.

Psychologically, the letter of intent helps to counteract what is known as buyer's remorse, in much the same way that securing a deposit from a potential tenant helps to prevent renters from backing out at the last minute.

Another common use of the letter of intent is to determine whether or not a property is available for sale and, if so, what price range is acceptable to the seller. Obviously, you would draft the letter and submit it to the seller under entirely different circumstances from those focused upon here.

If you did not know whether the property was available for sale, you would probably have to contact the property owner directly and offer a letter of intent to provide a very general indication of your interest and offer.

A typical letter of intent is a draft of an agreement between parties involved in negotiations relating to real estate; no uniform format binds the parties. The letter must be clear and concise. No points should be ambiguous.

It should say in the body of the text that the terms of the agreement, as laid out in the letter, are, at this point in the negotiations, non-binding. The general idea is to allow the other parties involved in the deal to get their heads around what they expect and what to see in the deal. If anything is missing, it will probably jump out at them when they review the letter of intent.

In most instances, you'll find that you can have a letter of intent drafted quickly since they are generally shorter and more informal than contracts. The final length of the letter will nonetheless be determined by the complexity of the deal that is under consideration.

You will be responsible for drafting the letter of intent when you are either the buyer or the party looking to lease a commercial space. For the most part, you will assign the task to your broker or agent, but you may also call upon your lawyer to draft the letter if they expect to represent you in the final sale transaction.

You should look for unambiguous terms and nonbinding language. The title, the first thing you'll see, should state either that it is a "nonbinding letter of intent" or that it is simply a "letter of intent." The confirmation that it represents a nonbinding agreement may be provided later on in the document. In rare cases, you may come across a letter of intent drafted as either a "term sheet" or as a "transaction outline." Both titles are acceptable if somewhat rarely used.

If not otherwise indicated in the title, the letter of intent should specifically state that the document is not legally binding. This provision should be included prominently somewhere in the document if it is not referred to directly in the title. Preferably, the phrase, "not legally binding" should be emphasized, either with capitalization, underlining, or bold text.

The nonbinding provision of the document should be indicated immediately above the signature lines for the document. Ambiguous phraseology such as "subject to legal documentation" or "subject to attorney approval" should certainly be avoided as this is a red flag for any savvy investor, buyer, or seller.

If there is any legally binding provision in your letter of intent – in some instances there are one or two – then these terms should be referred to and outlined in a section that is separate from the main nonbinding portion of the document. You may want to stipulate in the letter of intent that a property owner (prospective seller) should remove the property from the market while its sale is being considered as part of the deal outlined in the letter of intent.

These types of provisions must be placed in a separate section of the document to make it absolutely clear that it is an independent and legally binding obligation referred to in a document that otherwise contains nonbinding provisions for a prospective agreement.

The type of provisions you should generally include or look for in a letter of intent are as follows. First, it is very common to find what is called a "no shop" provision. This stipulates that either the seller or the landlord will not actively seek out other prospective buyers or tenants for a designated property while negotiations are underway to establish a binding contract. With this "no shop" provision, you will generally also include the condition about removing a property from the market while negotiations are taking place.

Since your hope is always to reach an agreement that will end up becoming legally binding, somewhere in a letter of intent that is designed as an agreement draft, you should include information about who is going to be responsible for the legal documentation of any agreement reached.

The points that will have to be considered include details like whose attorney will be responsible for drafting the documents, when the first draft should be completed, and who will be responsible for distributing the draft. It is also prudent to mention an intended deadline for any negotiations and also for the signing of a binding legal agreement that will facilitate the transfer of the property in question. All of these points will help to facilitate the cooperation of the other party involved in the deal.

Since most deals involve several parties, including not only the buyer and seller or landlord and tenant, but also the brokers, agents, and lawyers of the respective parties, it is extremely efficient practice to provide a comprehensive list of parties involved in the transaction along with any relevant information about their companies, contact information, mailing and physical addresses, phone and fax numbers, and email addresses.

The objective of your letter of intent is always to make sure that your purchase of a commercial real estate property – a gas station in this case - will go through smoothly. The more you can do to make the process as easy as possible for the other parties involved, the more likely you are to facilitate a close.

As part of a bigger and broader strategy for developing your gas station business, though, you should also have your second move thought out by the time that you have your letter of intent ready for distribution.

Options Contracts

One of your options to facilitate the purchase of a viable gas station site, as mentioned above, is to propose an options contract. This type of contract puts time on your side by allowing you to take control of a property with very little money down. It allows you the advantage of stretching out the payment terms so that you are not under great pressure to come up with a lot of cash fast.

When you are pretty much convinced that you want to buy a particular property, but the seller is asking a high price, the options contract may well be your most effective way of closing the deal to everyone's satisfaction. The seller basically allows time for you to come up with the money to close the deal while also allowing you to have control of the property in the interim period.

For a start-up gas station business enterprise, assuming you may not have funding immediately available; this can prove a particularly sensible purchasing option. You know you don't have to buy your gas station site, of course, but you should certainly be looking for ways to facilitate buying rather than leasing, if only because it offers better business security.

Split-Funding

Split-funding is halfway between several different buying and selling potions in the sense that it allows a buyer to meet a seller's demands but not necessarily all in one go. If your seller has terms that you are prepared but not necessarily equipped to accommodate, then the split funding may well be your best option for closing a deal.

Done right, split-funding allows you to manage your seller, accepting and acquiescing to their terms while also protecting or at least accounting for your own situation in a positive way.

A classic example of split funding is provided by the following instance. A buyer is very interested in purchasing a small-sized gas station with a convenience store attached. The seller is certainly open to the sale, but the seller wants to use the money they already have tied up in the business. Their key interest is to get cash relatively quickly so that their money used to buy the gas station in the first place is freed up.

The asking price for the gas station site, though, maybe slightly too high for you to manage all in one go, especially if you are looking to establish your gas station business from scratch; you may need to be investing some money in other resources for the business.

As the buyer, though, you may very well recognize the strengths of a particular site and set up for your business. You are also confident that you can transform the establishment so it will yield an extremely high return on anything you determine to invest. In one scenario, at least, you may want to invest a sizeable amount of money in the property to create a maximum yield scenario. The seller, on the other hand, wants to get all of their money that they put into the initial mortgage by the time that the deal closes. You may not be able to come up with the money that the seller wants in time for the closing but what you can do is suggest a deal based on split funding.

With split funding, you offer to assume financial responsibility for the mortgage that is already in place on the property and agree to pay the buyer half of what they are asking at the time that the sale is closed. The second half of the payment will be made eighteen months later, with an additional sum offered in the second installment of the payment as the interest owed.

In most scenarios where split financing applies, both the buyer and the seller are made happy by this agreement and, at the end of the eighteen-month period, after the closing of the deal and the first payment, if the buyer (you) fails to make the second payment owed, the property transfers back to the seller with relatively little long-term entanglement.

Floating Seller-Held Mortgages

When you have a motivated seller, the situation may well call for a very different financial deal structure. It may be suitable for you to offer what is known as a floating seller-held mortgage. These types of deals are relatively unknown outside of the industry. Many real estate investors have never heard of these types of deals. Nonetheless, a floating seller-held mortgage might help you to close a deal when you have a seller who, for one reason or another, is particularly interested in handing off their property quickly.

The basic principle of this type of deal is that you, as the buyer, finance the purchase of a property using the seller's assets. The seller serves as the primary lender for the transaction. Generally, the seller will assume a second mortgage for the buyer, and the buyer will work to pay off the mortgage loan with interest to the seller over a period upon which the parties both agree. Remember that the best instance in which to suggest this type of deal is going to be when you have a seller who is particularly keen to off-load their property.

Partial Release Agreement

Yet another option you might consider for your transactions is the partial release agreement. This technique will generally serve you best when you are dealing either with land or multifamily housing developers or development opportunities.

This type of arrangement allows you to develop a property before paying full price for it. In the case of a piece of land that might be developed into a gas station facility, for instance, you will be able to take control of the land with a small percentage of the sales price offered as a down payment. You will then be allowed to conduct the necessary development over a fixed time to enhance the value of the property.

In most instances, as the seller, you will agree to partial payments on an annual basis after making an initial deposit at the time of closing. You will pay the balance owed plus interest over a fixed length of time, and you will be provided with the legal power to conduct whatever developments you deem necessary on the property. The deal is referred to as partial release agreement because the seller will release portions of the property to you over the fixed payment period in accordance with how much you have paid to secure the property and meet your obligations as a buyer.

Engaging Your Seller

Regardless of the particular method you use to secure a deal on a gas station property, you have reviewed now the principle methods for buying and selling most forms of commercial real estate. You have options, in other words, and working knowledge that should help you to start your gas station business thinking outside of the box.

Information is usually something you can use this to your advantage. You can go to your seller and present them with a range of possible scenarios relating to the deal. Unless they are really not interested in selling, you are likely to win them over with one or other of these methods.

After discussing the options with the other party involved in the deal, you should be at the point that you have decided on a particular type of deal for the transaction itself. What becomes important, too, though, is whether the transaction option and its implications fit within the parameters of what you need for your gas station business.

However, when you have a method decided, upon you should certainly sit down with your attorney and start to consider the drafting of a legally binding contract. Most of the provisions of your deal will have been covered in the letter of intent, which should already have been submitted to the other parties involved in the deal. Now that you have agreed upon the type of deal, you're well on the way to having an agreement ready.

Working Out the Fine Print

A few things to bear in mind:

- Very few contracts are accepted in the first draft form

- Be prepared to sit down with your buyer or seller and their attorneys or brokers to negotiate particular provisions of your contract

- Don't be put off by redrafting, as it is a perfectly normal part of the process

As you become more experienced with business deals, you will feel increasingly confident about setting terms for payment agreements in exchange for paying the price desired by the owner in real estate transactions as well as most other business transactions you experience.

Let's say there is larger gas station lot that you'd really like to get your hands on. Perhaps it's in a great location, and it's within an area that you already have a sizeable interest, owning several other stations.

The seller of the property you want to buy is asking for $80,000, which you believe is a minimum of $20,000 more than what the property is actually worth, even to you.

You might have plans to modify the building somewhat. Perhaps you want to transform it into something of a garage or service station stop for those passing through the area. You know that this work is going to take at least a year; at the very least. You have to obtain the permits to make the changes, secure viable construction bids, and obtain financing.

When you have some experience under your belt, you'll automatically appreciate that time when a situation like this will work in your favor. First of all, you can offer the seller a percentage of their asking price as a 12-month option to buy. If you want to, you can also include as a term of the agreement that you should have the right to extend your option for another 12-months for a second payment as a portion of the asking price. If you decide to buy at the end of either the first year or the second year, then you will pay the remainder of the seller's asking price. If not, you will get out of the deal having spent only a portion.

You have several options available to you to work deals out to your advantage. First of all, you can look to secure a favorable deal for you. Rent adjustments are generally a part of every commercial lease. There are numerous different types of rent adjustments, including real estate tax adjustments, cost of living adjustments, common area maintenance, and percent gross sales adjustments.

Real estate tax adjustments are established on some leases when the seller/owner wants to collect increases in real estate tax over the amount assessed on the year that the lease was written. The owner offering the lease will have already taken into account the existing tax structure as part of the base rent but if there is a change in the value of the real estate tax; the owner will look to collect this.

Other leases established on larger properties including shopping centers or office buildings allow for taxes to be separated out as items charged to the lessee in accordance with the percentage of the property that it occupies as per the terms of the lease. The lessee, in this type of deal, is charged a percentage of the total assessed tax for each given year that corresponds to the percentage of the unit that they occupy.

A cost of living adjustment is another example of rental adjustments that can be used in commercial real estate agreements. This type of adjustment is a provision that is typically established in a separate paragraph of a given lease, although in some cases it is incorporated instead in a section of the lease agreement entitled "Lease Adjustments" or something different.

The cost of living adjustment is generally determined based on a formula that allows the person leasing out the property to increase the rent during the term of the lease, generally on an annual basis, as required.

To serve the interests of the person leasing the property, however, there is always a date set in the contract to determine when the lease may be adjusted in general. Notably, there is also a cap placed on the amount of an increase, such as 2.5% or 5%.

Common Area Maintenance Adjustments, commonly referred to as CAM, serve as a catch-all feature for most contracts designed to facilitate the lease of a property. These adjustments are charged to the tenants of commercial real estate property, and they tend to be all-inclusive. Of all the various types of rent adjustments applied during the leasing phase for commercial real estate, it is the CAM that serves as the most inclusive.

The CAM tends to cover possible outside cost ever to manage and maintain the property during the tenant's lease. The charges covered under this adjustment may include a reserve for replacement of major mechanical items, including air conditioning and heating equipment, lighting equipment costs, and other similar fees. These maintenance fees are generally established based on a percentage of the gross rent of the property. Where more than one tenant is leasing a property, the charges are divided equally among all of the tenants.

When all of the provisions have been addressed, you should be generally happy with the final legal document that you asked to sign. You should understand it fully, both in terms of what any legal jargon refers to and in terms of what your obligations are based on what each of the provisions means.

To close the deal, you are going to have to make sure that you, the other parties involved in the deal, and any outsiders who are serving as investors or guarantors, also know precisely what they are getting into.

Before anyone is asked to sign the final contract for a sale or for a lease agreement, be sure to do your due diligence and find out if any of the parties have any lingering concerns about how the deal with pan out. You can't please everyone, and just because someone isn't 100% happy with a deal doesn't mean that it isn't going to go through smoothly.

Nonetheless, work on maintaining a positive relationship with all concerned by facilitating open communication about the deal and taking advantage of opportunities to reassure them on its progress when the time comes. This personal and involved approach will close your deals 99% of the time.

Chapter 7: The Legal Stuff

The legal side of taking over a gas station business is daunting. The key to managing it is simply to be prepared, do your homework, have a business lawyer working with you, preferably one who has experience with gas station purchases or leases. Ideally, they should have worked with gas station owners on managing the various legal requirements for ownership and operation of the facility. Ask around, check references; see who in your community best fits the bill on this.

Once you have made the decision to go into business for yourself, though, you need to think about some of the legal implications of your decision as well as the particulars of what you are getting into industry-wise. You have to think about the type of company you are going to establish and exactly what form your business model is going to take.

Types of Companies

The first issue you need to address, from a legal standpoint, is the type of business you want to set up. Because you are going to be running a gas station – a particular kind of business – you need to set up a separate legal entity for the business. In other words, the option for you to go into business, as a gas station owner, in the capacity of a 'sole proprietor,' just isn't available to you.

What you're left with, then, are three general types of legal entities – the corporation, the limited liability company, or the partnership.

A. Corporations

There are two different types of corporations – S and C. The main difference between the two lies in taxes and shareholder relations. A corporation typically has corporate officers appointed by a board of directors, who are elected by shareholders. The shareholders also adopt corporate by-laws to provide structure and organizational guidance.

Some by-laws will be worded the same as the provisions in the charter that all corporations must file in their beginning stages. The corporate charter, also referred to as Articles of Incorporation, outlines the structure of the organization, its rights, and restrictions. It must be submitted for approval by the secretary of state in the corporation's home state. The charter will either be approved, or it will be sent back with suggested changes.

Subchapter S corporations are a more popular option for small businesses and family-owned companies. S corporation status is available for the free-standing U.S. - based companies with fewer than 100 U.S. - based shareholders, only one class of stock, and at least 20 percent of total business revenue generated in the U.S.

Shareholders in S corporations are viewed more as partners rather than owners, meaning the business will not be subject to double taxation. Shareholders in S corporations use their individual tax filings to report all their income or loss related to the business. C corporations, on the other hand, must pay taxes on business income and then a second time on the net profits distributed as dividends to shareholders.

Aside from those differences, both types of corporations are fairly similar. A corporation seeking subchapter S status must first file a charter for general corporation status with the Office of the Secretary of State. Later, a Form 2553 may be filed with the IRS to obtain subchapter S status, but this must be done within 75 days of being in business or within the first 75 days of the company's fiscal year. All shareholders must agree to adopt the subchapter S status and, if approved, the status will remain in effect until canceled. The process of incorporation can get much more complicated, depending largely on individual state laws, so companies seriously considering this step should consult their Secretary of State's Office for more detailed information.

B. Limited Liability Company (LLC)

Forming a limited liability company, or LLC, is not a terribly complicated procedure. In fact, it is only a matter of a few hundred dollars and a small amount of paperwork. Instead of filing Articles of Incorporation with the Secretary of State's

Office, a business owner would need to file Articles of Organization with the LLC filing office. This document is also sometimes referred to as a certificate of formation or certificate of organization.

LLC filing offices often have forms that make the process of creating Articles of Organization as simple as checking a few boxes. Whereas paperwork related to the formation of a corporation must be filed in the corporation's home state, paperwork related to the formation of an LLC must be filed in the state where the LLC intends to conduct business.

There are many benefits of an LLC. It allows a limitless number of owners who may be from any nation, unlike an S corporation. With LLCs, double taxation and corporate taxes are non-issues because business income and losses are reported directly on the owners' personal tax filings. In most states, LLC owners cannot be personally sued for anything related to the LLC unless criminal wrongdoing is involved, at which point the LLC legal protections disappear.

C. Partnership

The IRS defines a partnership as —the relationship between two or more persons who join to carry on a trade or business. In this case, Articles of Partnership are often created by the partners and filed with the clerk of the local court. Neither of these steps are legal requirements, but they are common-sense steps to outline clearly and make a public record of the physical contributions and general responsibilities of each party.

There can be different types of partners in a business, distinguished in a couple of ways. The first distinction is whether a partner is a general partner or a limited partner.

A general partner is publicly involved in the business and its daily operations. A limited partner is not and mainly serves as a source of capital funding.

The second distinction comes down to involvement in the business. The active partner helps run the business, which may or may not be public knowledge. A secret partner helps run the business, which is not public knowledge. The silent partner does not help run the business but can be publicly associated with it.

Partnerships feature lower tax rates and limited government interference in daily operations. However, partnerships are usually short-lived, there is a great chance of conflict between the partners over money and other business matters, and partners are personally liable for the business debt. Limited partners, on the other hand, have no personal responsibility for the business debt so long as they were not involved in managing the business.

Incorporating Your Business

Depending on the type of business being formed, the following information is required in the paperwork.

Articles of Incorporation:

- Corporation name, purpose or function, date of formation, business address, incorporator(s), capital structure, capital requirement, preemptive rights, initial directors

- Internal affairs charter changes

- LLC

- Partnership (filing not legally required)

Most articles of incorporation also include:

- A listing of the state in which the company is being incorporated

- A determination of the duration of the corporation or partnership

- A statement about the purpose of the corporation

- Details on the powers of the corporation

- An indication of the initial registered agent and registered office address of the corporation

- A statement of acceptance of the role of the registered agent

Articles of incorporation should also detail the following:

- The principal office address and mailing address of the corporation

- Information on the authorized shares of stock of the corporation, a description of the class of stock, information on the par values of shares

- Information on the initial directors and officers of the corporation

- Indication of corporate bylaws to be adopted

- Information on a plan for the dissolution of the corporation

- A statement indemnifying the officers and directors

The articles should also list basic information on the person undertaking the incorporation and a valid address for correspondence. I am attaching a sample LLC formation document so you can get an idea of how they look (See Appendix).

Once you have managed the basics of incorporating your business and determining what structure it will take, you will need to look into the necessary licensing and certification responsibilities for gas stations and, if you are selling certain kinds of goods at your station, for other types of retailers too.

Understanding State and Local Regulatory Licenses

Dotting the I's and crossing the T's for your gas station business is going to require a lot of hoop-jumping and dealing with seemingly redundant formalities. Unfortunately, there is just no way around the legal parameters when it comes to setting up a gas station business.

You are dealing with big industry, even if you are just dealing with the suppliers of gas. Because of the potential safety risks and other considerations of storing, it is vitally important that you have all of the necessary paperwork in place and that you jump through all of the appropriate hoops.

You are going to need to look into the specific state requirements based on the location of your business but here is a basic list of the type of licenses and certifications you should expect to have to obtain.

City or county regulations that may apply:

- Building and Construction Permits: Required for all new and remodeling construction.

- Business License (Business Tax Registration): Any person or entity carrying on a trade or business may need to obtain a business license, use and occupancy permit or business tax certificate including those that are located outside the city limits but perform services for customers inside the city limits.

- Fire Prevention Information/Inspection: Businesses may be subject to a yearly inspection of the facility. An annual fee may be charged depending on the type of business.

- Hazardous Materials/Underground Storage Tank Permit: May need to obtain a permit if storing any hazardous materials in aboveground containers/tanks or in underground storage tanks within incorporated city limits.

- - Businesses that store hazardous materials may need to file a hazardous materials business plan.

  - Separate permits may be required for installing and closing storage tanks and storage facilities.

  - Contaminated sites from leaking underground storage tanks that are closed may require remediation oversight.

- Industrial Wastewater Discharge Permit: May be required if a facility discharges industrial wastewater into the sewer.

- Land Use Permits/Zoning: Permitted uses, development regulations, zone change, variance, and conditional use permit.

- Special Permits/Licenses: Requirements vary by area, but you should check with your local city or county council to determine if you need a special permit or license.

- Business Property Statement: Businesses are required to report all equipment, fixtures, supplies, and leasehold improvements held for business use.

- Fictitious Business Name: When a business goes by any name other than the owner's real name, the business operates under a "fictitious name" and must file a "Doing Business As" statement.

- Hazardous Waste Generator Permit: May need to obtain a permit if generating hazardous waste from normal operations of a business. A generator identification number and a taxpayer identification number may be required from state or federal governments.

- Health Permit: Required for all retail markets, bars, restaurants, catering trucks, and mobile food preparation vehicles, health food stores, temporary event food booths, vending machines.

- Hazardous Materials Permit may be required.

- On-Site Hazardous Waste Treatment Permit.

- Weights and Measures Device Registration: Businesses commercially using scales, fuel pumps, electronic or manual price lookup scanner devices, meters, or other measuring devices may have to ensure proper calibration and pass inspections.

Regional Regulations that May Apply

- Authority to Construct/Permit to Operate: For stationary sources of air emissions from specific types of equipment, industrial processes, paints and solvents, and some consumer products.

State Regulations that May Apply

- Air Tank Permits.

- Automobile Repair Dealer Registration: May be required to perform automotive repairs, including mobile mechanics.

- Corporation, Company, or Partnership Filings.

- Discrimination Law: Harassment or discrimination in employment is prohibited if it is based on a person's race, ancestry, national origin, color, sex (including pregnancy), sexual orientation, religion, physical disability (including AIDS), mental disability, marital status, medical condition (cured cancer), and refusal of family care leave.

    - The above information must usually be stated in employment notices and provided to employees or the relevant laws presented to employees or posted prominently within

- o Employers must also provide notice of an employee's right to request pregnancy disability leave or transfer, as well as notice to request a family and medical care leave.

- Industrial Activities Storm Water General Permit: National Pollutant Discharge Elimination System (NPDES) General Permit No. CAS000001 includes waste discharge requirements for discharges of stormwater associated with industrial activities, excluding construction activities.

- Occupational Safety and Health Information: Businesses with employees must prepare an Injury and Illness Prevention Plan. The state provides a no-fee consultation service to assist employers with preventing unsafe working conditions and workplace hazards.

- Registration Form for Employers.

- Sales & Use Permit (Seller's Permit): All businesses selling or leasing tangible property usually have to have and prominently display this permit.

- State EPA Identification Number: Usually required of businesses that generate, surrender to be transported, transport, treat, or dispose of hazardous waste.

- State Income Tax Information: Businesses may have to obtain the appropriate state income tax forms from the Franchise Tax Board.

- Underground Storage Tank Fee: If you own an underground storage tank, you may have to register with state authorities and pay a fee for various petroleum products placed into your tank.

- Wage/Hour Laws: Businesses with employees must comply with laws establishing minimum standards for wages, hours, and working conditions.

- Waste Discharge Requirements (WDR's): Any facility or activity that discharges, or proposes to discharge, waste that may affect groundwater quality or from which waste may be discharged in a diffused manner (e.g., erosion from soil disturbance) may have to obtain waste discharge requirements.

- Workers' Compensation Information: Businesses with employees may have to maintain Workers' Compensation Insurance coverage on either a self-insured basis, or provided through a commercial carrier, or state-run Workers' Compensation Insurance Fund.

Federal Regulations (for Employers)

- Employer Identification Number (EIN or SSN).

- Proof of Residency Requirement: Employees hired after November 6, 1986, must provide proof of eligibility to work in the United States.

- E- Verify the newest employment eligibility verification site.

Underground Storage Tanks Registrations

UST refers to Underground Storage Tanks. When they contain motor fuel, USTs are subject to heavy regulation at both a state and federal level. Being in compliance with UST related regulations, ensuring that you have the proper registration and certifications, as a gas station owner, are crucial.

The best way to understand the registration requirements is to go to the website of the Environmental Protection Agency or EPA. On this page, http://www.epa.gov/oust/overview.htm, you can find most of what you need to know about federal and even state regulations for USTs. At the very least, you get a good overview and have access to appropriate links to find more information about the regulations that apply at a federal and state level.

Make sure you follow through on the requirements laid out in the regulations. Specifically, you are required to report "suspected releases" as well as "spills and overfills."

In fact, pay particular attention to Subpart C-General Operating Requirements, featured below.

§ 280.30 Spill and overfill control.

(a) Owners and operators must ensure that releases due to spilling or overfilling do not occur. The owner and operator must ensure that the volume available in the tank is greater than the volume of product to be transferred to the tank before the transfer is made and that the transfer operation is monitored constantly to prevent overfilling and spilling.

(b) The owner and operator must report, investigate, and clean up any spills and overfills in accordance with § 280.53.

§ 280.31 Operation and maintenance of corrosion protection.

All owners and operators of steel UST systems with corrosion protection must comply with the following requirements to ensure that releases due to corrosion are prevented for as long as the UST system is used to store regulated substances:

(a) All corrosion protection systems must be operated and maintained to continuously provide corrosion protection to the metal components of that portion of the tank and piping that routinely contain regulated substances and are in contact with the ground.

(b) All UST systems equipped with cathodic protection systems must be inspected for proper operation by a qualified cathodic protection tester in accordance with the following requirements:

(1) Frequency. All cathodic protection systems must be tested within 6 months of installation and at least every 3 years thereafter or according to another reasonable time frame established by the implementing agency; and

(2) Inspection criteria. The criteria that are used to determine that cathodic protection is adequate as required by this section must be in accordance with a code of practice developed by a nationally recognized association.

Note: National Association of Corrosion Engineers Standard RP-02-85, "Control of External Corrosion on Metallic Buried,

Partially Buried, or Submerged Liquid Storage Systems," may be used to comply with paragraph (b)(2) of this section.

(c) UST systems with impressed current cathodic protection systems must also be inspected every 60 days to ensure the equipment is running properly.

(d) For UST systems using cathodic protection, records of the operation of the cathodic protection must be maintained (in accordance with § 280.34) to demonstrate compliance with the performance standards in this section. These records must provide the following:

(1) The results of the last three inspections required in paragraph (c) of this section; and

(2) The results of testing from the last two inspections required in paragraph (b) of this section.

§ 280.32 Compatibility.

Owners and operators must use an UST system made of or lined with materials that are compatible with the substance stored in the UST system.

Note: Owners and operators storing alcohol blends may use the following codes to comply with the requirements of this section:

(a) American Petroleum Institute Publication 1626, "Storing and Handling Ethanol and Gasoline-Ethanol Blends at Distribution Terminals and Service Stations"; and

(b) American Petroleum Institute Publication 1627, "Storage and Handling of Gasoline-Methanol/Cosolvent Blends at Distribution Terminals and Service Stations."

§ 280.33 Repairs allowed.

Owners and operators of UST systems must ensure that repairs will prevent releases due to structural failure or corrosion as long as the UST system is used to store regulated substances. The repairs must meet the following requirements:

(a) Repairs to UST systems must be properly conducted in accordance with a code of practice developed by a nationally recognized association or an independent testing laboratory.

(b) Repairs to fiberglass-reinforced plastic tanks may be made by the manufacturer's authorized representatives or in accordance with a code of practice developed by a nationally recognized association or an independent testing laboratory.

(c) Metal pipe sections and fittings that have released product as a result of corrosion or other damage must be replaced. Fiberglass pipes and fittings may be repaired in accordance with the manufacturer's specifications.

(d) Repaired tanks and piping must be tightness tested in accordance with § 280.43(c) and § 280.44(b) within 30 days following the date of the completion of the repair except as provided in paragraphs (d) (1) through (3), of this section:

(1) The repaired tank is internally inspected in accordance with a code of practice developed by a nationally recognized association or an independent testing laboratory; or

(2) The repaired portion of the UST system is monitored monthly for releases in accordance with a method specified in § 280.43 (d) through (h); or

(3) Another test method is used that is determined by the implementing agency to be no less protective of human health and the environment than those listed above.

(e) Within 6 months following the repair of any cathodically protected UST system, the cathodic protection system must be tested in accordance with § 280.31 (b) and (c) to ensure that it is operating properly.

(f) UST system owners and operators must maintain records of each repair for the remaining operating life of the UST system that demonstrate compliance with the requirements of this section.

§ 280.34 Reporting and recordkeeping.

Owners and operators of UST systems must cooperate fully with inspections, monitoring and testing conducted by the implementing agency, as well as requests for document submission, testing, and monitoring by the owner or operator pursuant to section 9005 of Subtitle I of the Resource Conservation and Recovery Act, as amended.

(a) Reporting. Owners and operators must submit the following information to the implementing agency:

(1) Notification for all UST systems (§ 280.22), which includes certification of installation for new UST systems (§ 280.20(e)),

(2) Reports of all releases including suspected releases (§ 280.50), spills and overfills (§ 280.53), and confirmed releases (§ 280.61);

(3) Corrective actions planned or taken including initial abatement measures (§ 280.62), initial site characterization (§ 280.63), free product removal (§ 280.64), investigation of soil and ground-water cleanup (§ 280.65), and corrective action plan (§ 280.66); and

(4) A notification before permanent closure or change-in-service (§ 280.71).

(b) Recordkeeping. Owners and operators must maintain the following information:

(1) A corrosion expert's analysis of site corrosion potential if corrosion protection equipment is not used (§ 280.20(a)(4); § 280.20(b)(3)).

(2) Documentation of operation of corrosion protection equipment (§ 280.31);

(3) Documentation of UST system repairs (§ 280.33(f));

(4) Recent compliance with release detection requirements (§ 280.45); and

(5) Results of the site investigation conducted at permanent closure (§ 280.74).

(c) Availability and Maintenance of Records. Owners and operators must keep the records required either:

(1) At the UST site and immediately available for inspection by the implementing agency; or

(2) At a readily available alternative site and be provided for inspection to the implementing agency upon request.

(3) In the case of permanent closure records required under § 280.74, owners and operators are also provided with the additional alternative of mailing closure records to the implementing agency if they cannot be kept at the site or an alternative site as indicated above.

Resellers Certificate from State Department of Revenue

In every state, every retailer is usually issued a sales tax certificate with which you can buy products and merchandise at a wholesale price without paying sales tax, provided you will sell those merchandise and products through your store and collect sales tax where applicable.

The best way to determine the certification and licensing requirements correctly is to contact an experienced business CPA. You should also visit your state website to find links to pertinent information from the state department of revenue.

For instance, the state government website for Pennsylvania is pa.gov. Very likely, you are going to need to obtain certification and licensing to operate your gas station within the law.

Employment Identification Numbers

When you incorporate your business, you receive a taxpayer ID number from the federal government (the IRS).

Your EIN, Federal Employer Identification Number, or FTIN, Federal Tax Identification Number, is the number that you will use when filing taxes for your business and undertaking such tasks as hiring paying an employee of your company.

To find out how to obtain an EIN, go to http://www.irs.gov/Businesses/Small-Businesses-&-Self-Employed/Employer-ID-Numbers-(EINs)-.

You (Or Your Company) as an Employer

The second you employ someone to work for you, you need to go to work figuring out the tax ramifications. The first question to ask yourself: is my employee actually an employee or are they, independent contractors, instead?

More likely than not, you are going to be hiring bona fide employees at your gas station. If you find yourself working with independent contractors, you will need to look into your tax responsibilities separately. This is the IRS link to Forms and Associated Taxes for Independent Contractors.

With employees versus contractors, your tax responsibilities include withholding, depositing, reporting, and paying employment taxes.

Basic Paperwork for Employers

We will talk about how you find the right person for the job in part II. Before you hire anyone, you need to verify a few details about them. The first thing you must verify is that your new employee is legally eligible to work in the United States. Make sure your employees fill out, Form I-9, Employment Eligibility Verification when they come to work for you.

To manage your various responsibilities to the IRS, your employee needs to give you their social security number as well. You will need this and their full legal name to enter into a Form W-2. Note that this requirement is in place for both resident and nonresident alien employees as well as citizens.

Ask your employee to show you their social security card and make a point of photocopying it for your records.

For the purposes of effective record keeping, you should also record each new employee's name and social security number from their social security card.

It is important that you can distinguish between a social security number (SSN) and an ITIN. An ITIN is only available to resident and nonresident aliens who are not eligible for U.S. employment. An ITIN is a 9-digit number, beginning with the number "9" and is formatted like an SSN (NNN-NN-NNN). Everyone you hire should have a valid social security number, period. Anyone eligible to work in the US can apply for an SSN easily by finding their local SS office.

The main reason you need your employees' SSN is that you handle paying certain taxes on their behalf.

Payroll Withholding Requirements

You need to withhold a certain amount from your employees' wages to pay taxes, for which you need a Form W-4, Employee's Withholding Allowance Certificate on file for every one of your employees.

All new employees need to give you a signed Form W-4 when they start work, to be effective with the first wage payment. Employees who can claim exemption from income tax withholding must indicate this on their W-4.

To help yourself and your employees keep track of withholding, you can use the withholding allowance calculator in addition to the Form W-4 worksheet to make sure that your calculations for withholding are accurate.

My advice is you should hire a payroll service or hire an accountant or a CPA who can help you with your payroll needs since this a complex and time sensitive matter. I have always handed this duty over to my CPA.

In addition to withholding, you are going to need to consider certain employee benefits.

Fringe Benefits

Fringe benefits are included in an employee's gross income with some exception. Benefits are subject to withholding and employment taxes as well, which is why you may need an accountant on retainer to avoid mistakes.

Fringe benefits can include cars and flights on aircraft that the employer provides, free or discounted commercial flights, vacations, discounts on property or services, memberships in country clubs or other social clubs, corporate gym memberships, and tickets to entertainment or sporting events. If you become particularly enterprising with your gas station business, you could easily find yourself providing some of these benefits, so it is better to be aware of the law. Ignorance is so rarely a defense.

To figure out the taxation of fringe benefits, you have to include the value of the item based on fair market value, listing the amount by which the fair market value of the benefits is more than the sum of what the employee pays for anything, also allowing for any amount that the law excludes.

The best source of information on fringe benefits, and how they impact accounting and taxation for employers are Publication 15-B, Employers' Tax Guide to Fringe Benefits.

Unemployment Insurance

Unemployment insurance is something you are going to have to know about as well. The Federal Unemployment Tax Act (FUTA) provides for payments of the unemployment compensation to workers who have lost their jobs. As an employer, you will likely have to pay both a federal and a state unemployment tax.

For more information on this, go to the Department of Labor's Web site under the listing of Unemployment Insurance Tax Topics.

Workers' Compensation

Four major disability compensation programs provide wage replacement benefits, medical treatment, vocational rehabilitation, and other benefits to federal workers or their dependents. The Office of Workers' Compensation Programs (OWCP) manages this for federal employers, and you can get a sense of what compensation can look like by checking out this resource.

Private employers need to know about workers' compensation because there are certain liabilities with work-related accidents or on-the-job injuries.

Contact your [state workers' compensation board](#) to determine what workers' compensation programs look like in your state and talk to your business attorney to get a sense of what programs or insurance you can obtain for your business.

Health Plans

Providing access to health insurance programs helps your employees and their families to address basic medical needs and be proactive about their health. If you pay for the cost of an accident or a health insurance plan for your employees, these benefits are not subject to Social Security, Medicare, or FUTA taxes, or federal income tax withholding according to the IRS. In fact, they are also not considered wages in most cases, although there are some exceptions.

For more information about workers rights concerning health care benefits, check out the Department of Labor's [Health Benefits Under the Consolidated Omnibus Budget Reconciliation ACT (COBRA)](#). You should also check for regulations impacting your state.

Basic Record Keeping

With the numerous demands to retain information and the need to calculate different benefits and tax payments for employees, it is extremely important to keep detailed records. The further benefit of record-keeping, of course, is that you can actually monitor the progress of your business.

At the very least, you need financial records including copies of receipts and employee payments and benefits, to prepare your tax returns and support items reported on tax returns.

For tax purposes, the type of business you are in impacts the records you need to keep. Choose whatever kind of record-keeping system works for you and your business and make sure that you are diligent about maintaining the records and storing them.

The length of time you need to keep financial records depends on the nature of the records. At a minimum, you should keep any records that impact federal taxes and all records of employment taxes for at least five years.

Generally, you need to keep track of all supporting documents for purchases, sales, payrolls, and other transactions related to your business.

The burden of proof is upon you when it comes to expenses that are deducted from your tax payments and any other calculations made on your tax returns. Being thorough and diligent about your record-keeping will, at the very least, save you a headache down the road.

Part II

Managing Your Gas Station Business

Chapter 8: Becoming Oriented Post-Purchase

Now you are the proud owner of a gas station business.

Congratulations!

If this is your first time owning a business or your first time owning property, it probably feels great and just a little bit scary to have closed the deal.

Okay, it probably feels very scary.

You not only have a tremendous opportunity before you, but you also have a tremendous responsibility. The best thing you can do right now is taking a big deep breath.

As tempting as it is, you probably should avoid mucking in right after closing your real estate deal. Don't go and take a five-week vacation or anything, but do give yourself a day to clear your head.

Once you have signed the papers and the deal is done, thank your lawyer, thank the seller, head out for a mini-celebration (treat yourself), and then take a day to just relax and think about other things, spend some time with friends and family. Distinguish the sales process from the ownership process. You have a lot of work to do, and you need to do it with a clear head – the head of a business owner.

When your day is up, you have to hit the ground running, so enjoy yourself, have a break, but don't get too comfortable in 'relaxation' mode.

To manage your new business smoothly, you are going to have to develop military-like precision when it comes to planning and strategizing. You are also going to have to learn, as many business people struggle to, actually, what it takes to be an effective business owner.

The last thing you should be doing, assuming you want to grow your gas station business, is putting out fires (the metaphorical kind). You need to establish your business system in the early days of operation to allow yourself the freedom to (almost) always focus on the big picture.

Giving yourself some space after the sale is one way to start letting that be your perspective – the big picture part. Another couple of things you can do, as we will discuss in part two: strategize and plan effectively, follow key principles of marketing, hire good staff, and constantly check yourself to see how you can improve.

Without further ado, let's get to work discussing how you can make your business run smoothly and at a growing profit.

Figuring Out Your First Move

As you will notice in the next couple of chapters, there is a necessary emphasis on marketing and sales strategies when you get started with the management of your gas station business. A careful focus on these two businesses activates – absolutely crucial to success in just about every industry out there – helped me achieve millions in sales with my several gas stations.

Before you even think about marketing and sales, though, which is going to require you to take a careful look at the layout of your store to figure out where different products should be positioned, you need to begin to think about what products you are going to be selling and how you are going to set about branding your business.

What is branding?

Branding is basically the process of creating an identity or your company, an identity by which your company can be assessed and checked. Although it is not immediately obvious how branding impacts gas station businesses, the truth is that branding impacts just about any business, including gas station businesses.

People have certain values that they attach to gas station companies, including, for instance, BP or Mobile.

The far broader concept of these brands includes just about anything to do with the public image of these companies, what happens with these companies on the stock market, what happens to them in broader events.

The BP oil spill was a major PR issue for BP, and doubtless impacted how people registered the BP gas stations. At least a few people are going to think twice about buying BP gas at the pump. Perhaps a few even drove an extra mile or in a different direction, via a different route, to find a different gas station. You get the idea.

Now, there are options as far as branding within your corporate company. If you have a franchise that is part of a larger gas station chain, you have some limitations on your branding options. You have to work within the image of the franchise owner. On the other hand, you can use the broader brand, the larger company image, to engage your community. Use the established brand to build a great reputation and credibility.

If you have an independent gas station, you can work on branding from scratch, which can be more work but has other benefits. You have greater flexibility when you brand yourself.

How do you go about branding?

Well, a lot of it comes down to the details of your presentation. The look and feel of your store will support your brand. If you are going for a modern brand, let it be clean and uncluttered.

If you are going for a more old school, traditional-looking gas station, see what elements you can incorporate into your store, what little details you can use to enhance the idea.

Branded vs. Unbranded Gasoline

In addition to the furnishings of your store, one of the details that are going to impact your brand is the gasoline you sell.

Gasoline can be branded or unbranded, and choosing between the two isn't just a dilemma limited to food and clothes.

Obviously, if you have a gas franchise or if you are aiming for a gas franchise, you have Shell, Texaco, Chevron, Mobil, BP, Marathon, Fina and so many more to choose from. Yes, when you use these brands, they have a reputation and an established image. Not to mention they are known to motorists, and there are going to be at least some enthusiasts for each of the various brands.

Unbranded gasoline exists, too, and it has the pretty obvious advantage of being a lot cheaper, by comparison, than the branded options.

One of the quality drawbacks, though, is that unbranded gasoline doesn't contain the same additives as the branded fuels. It is available at a little cheaper cost because no cleaning additive added to that fuel and secondly no-name brand is attached to that fuel. But it is cheaper. If you are branding yourself to be the Wal-Mart of gas stations, the value for money will be quite well received by your target audience. You won't be losing anything. In fact, you probably gain a few points. Just remember when it comes to motor fuel, cheaper doesn't always mean inferior quality.

Aim to target the more established car owners, though, the middle to upper-class folks, professionals, you are probably not going to have the same response. In fact, you might alienate a few of them, especially the car enthusiasts who know enough about the pros and cons of branded versus unbranded gasoline without being told.

Before deciding on the brand of fuel look around in your city and state and find out which are the strongest brands in terms of the number of open stations for that specific brand, this way you will know which company or brand has more credit card base in your area which can help you grown very rapidly. Additionally you also have to decide if you want to carry diesel and marine fuel, and if you are in or around a rural farming community, you may also want to consider carrying off-road diesel for farm equipment.

Once you have addressed this issue, you can start to work out the building of your gas station company and brand from the inside out. It shouldn't be too long before the pieces fall into place when you have this first problem squared away.

Determining Your Opening Day

Another problem to address early on is your timeframe. There is going to be sometime between the days you sign on the dotted line to actually purchase your gas station and the day on which you actually open your doors to customers.

The exact timeframe is something to consider and something that will set the frame for a lot of your activities. Not a bad thing.

You should think about what day is going to be best to open your doors. Depending on any promotional activities you might have planned – like a grand opening day (always a good idea) – you should think about the events you plan on coordinating around your open day and what else people might be doing or thinking about doing instead of attending and checking out what your store has to offer.

Picking your opening day requires some planning also in terms of weather and the time of year. Let's assume you are going to do the smart thing and have a grand opening. It makes sense to have a kind of barbecue event if you are opening in the summer or even in the late spring, and the weather is likely to be good. You should probably have a rain check day just in case, but the odds are that you can pull that kind of event off, and it will have a positive impact.

In the winter months or the fall, though, what can you do? Perhaps check out the events going on in your community and see what other businesses are planning. If you are opening around Thanksgiving or Halloween, perhaps consider planning an opening event that centers around one of these holidays. They have numerous themes and nuances that you can work around. Even Christmas or New Year work well for Grand Opening themes. You should also consider what promotions you can run at a premium to get people through the doors.

So much of this is going to be determined by the day you open your door. Working back from that date, you can also start to figure out the other timeframes and schedules for hiring staff, ordering supplies, working on any paperwork, and figuring out how to fit everything into place.

Chapter 9: Market Research as the First Step to Management

It might seem a little odd to begin a section on business management with a chapter on market research. For any business, an understanding of the market is crucial. If you don't know your market, you don't know your business. Your market defines your business. It tells you what your customers want from you, what they are interested in that you might be able to sell them, how you could improve your service; all that. This is what market research comes down to, and it needs to be an ongoing process.

How, though, do you conduct market research for your gas station business?

The simple answer is that you establish a process for obtaining feedback from your customers and for otherwise monitoring what your customers are buying from you and your competitors.

The more complex answer to that question involves consideration of what exactly is involved in achieving each of these objectives – how do you go about obtaining feedback from your customers? How can you effectively monitor their activities and their buying habits at your facility and at your competitors' facilities?

We will address these issues in this chapter.

Once you have your business established, and you are ready to open the doors, you should have at least some of the initial information you will need to start assessing who your customers are and how you might go about obtaining feedback and updated information on their activities and interests affecting your business.

Questions You Need to Ask (And Answer) Regularly

The first element of research always comes down to what you are trying to discover. In this instance, the key element of your market research comes down to a single question: how can I sell more?

There are two general ways to sell more. One is to bring in more customers, and the other is to bring in your customers more frequently.

The goal of your market research is to determine how you can a) secure more customers and how you can b) bring in existing customers more regularly (generate more repeat business).

Ideally, you want to aim at doing both of these things.

The key to finding out how you go about doing them? Make sure you ask the right questions.

Survey your customers. What do your existing customers want to buy in addition to gasoline? What actually makes them stop at your shop versus the other two down the street?

When you have answers to these questions and others like them, you can start to play out what type of activities might work to draw attention to your gas station and bring customers through your doors.

One of the biggest challenges, of course, is identifying marketing strategies that are appropriate for your business.

Gas stations are great businesses, but they are by no means typical in terms of how they operate and what they do. In fact, they are rather unique in the sense that they are representative of a very particular industry; they are the front-line representatives of the gas companies and even oil companies to some degree. It's not like you go to a gas station for the quality of gas, either.

Chances are you go to a gas station for one of two reasons. Either you go because it is the most convenient option you have, or you go because there is some aspect of the customer service. But how do you tap into this from a marketing perspective to get more foot traffic into your gas station store?

How about a free car wash promo? Buy a tank of gas, get your car washed. Something like this could get a lot of people showing up on your parking lot, and it's not just about balancing the cost of a car wash (for you) with the cost of a tank of gas.

People who are likely stopping at your station for a car wash and a tank of gas are at least going to come inside your store and buy a cup of coffee or a coke. You never know, if you are selling fast food and snacks, you might find you sell a lot of those things, too.

Rather than a car wash, how about discounts on some of your food and deli items? Check out some local popular chain stores like Circle K's or 7-11 and their loyalty programs. They constantly have deals that they advertise pretty heavily at their stores. There's always a sign in the window saying it's 3 for 2 on 12 packs of soda or similar.

The best way to gauge what is going to work for your station is to know your market and do some specific research into what types of deals and promos are really going to get people going. Market research will serve you well with this kind of thing.

Questions you need to ask would be along these lines:

- How often do your customers visit gas stations?

- What factors into the decision to go to a particular gas station?

- Are you loyal to a particular gas station or chain?

- Would you be interested in trying out a different gas station?

- Would you be interested in using a gas station that offered customer loyalty points and discounts?

- What is the most common reason (other than to get gas) for visiting a gas station? (e.g., milk, coffee, newspaper)

- What kind of promotional offers or events would entice you to visit a new gas station site? (E.g. free car wash for a tank of gas, barbecue, etc.).

Get answers to this kind of questions, along with demographic information, and you should be set to go.

Organizing Market Research Information

To get things started with your market research, consider what market information you have already. You should, as we have already suggested, have access to demographics information on the local population – people within the vicinity of your gas station facility. You should also have a good idea of the traffic count for the streets on which your business is located.

These two pieces of information are crucial.

You are also going to want to get a sense of your customers' buying habits. Where do they shop for milk most often? How often do they go to the grocery store? How often do they get gas? What newspapers do they read and do they have a subscription? How often do they actually buy a newspaper in-store?

You have to tailor your market research information based on demographics and based on what sales data you might have from the previous station owner. You also have to factor in your gut feeling as to what the trends and patterns are for gas stations in your particular region.

Marketing Tools and Schedules

How are you going to collect information and at what intervals?

It's not enough to know the questions you need the answers to. You actually have to go about getting the answers.

How are you going to do that?

Perhaps the best strategy is to have a focus group. Invite some customers to join you for maybe half an hour to talk about some of the things they like and don't like about gas stations in the area.

Alternatively, (and this might be a little easier to organize) have your customers complete a survey on gas stations in the area, how they tend to use them, and what improvements they would like to see.

Analyzing Marketing Data and Acting On It

Depending on the data collection tools you use, you have to develop a strategy for data analysis and appropriate follow-through.

Data collection should be determined by the goals you have for your marketing. For instance, if you want to increase sales or increase brand recognition/loyalty to your company. These are really the only main goals a single gas station should have. You should go about collecting and analyzing data about the number of 'conversions' or sales.

What are the visitors to sales ratio? How many of the people walking through your door or onto your lot actually go ahead and buy from you? How many of those who buy gasoline actually go into your store and buy something other than gas?

You are going to need to collect this information through some form of tracking in addition to the survey-type data we have suggested as a basis for helping to improve your customer experience. Having these numbers will help you track improvement over time.

Because you are not dealing with data as easily managed as online traffic and site conversions, you might want to consider hiring out some of this market research, at least in the beginning, while you have a lot of other things to manage.

However, since you're tracking sales and inventory data anyway for accounting purposes, you may find that a bit of effort gets you a sound system for managing the marketing side of things too. Some of the time, at least, success will come to persistence.

You are going to want to properly review your sales and marketing data – customers through the door, dollars spent on advertising, special promotions, and their impact – for a couple of months, at least.

You should also think about creating a consistent marketing calendar with special events marked.

The more time you spend planning out the details of a marketing plan, the better prepared you'll be when it's time to open the doors and put your plan into effect.

Chapter 10: Your First Days of Business: Putting a Plan Into Action

Now that you have a program for your market research, you have what you need to open the doors to your business. As soon as your first customer steps onto your property, you have the means to monitor their impact on your business, and you have the opportunity to learn and do better.

The first day of business should be the model for every other usual day. Try to minimize the surprises that hit you and your staff. Don't fly blind. Instead, before you open your doors, make sure you have conducted some kind of dress rehearsal for your business.

Pre-Opening Checklist

Here's what you need to check and double-check before you open your doors on the first day:

1. **Are you up to code with everything?**

    Regulations and legal requirements play a substantial role in the management of a gas station. There's no getting around this, and any corner-cutting in this area is very likely to cost you not only a lot of money but also a lot of time to fix.

Before you open doors to customers, make absolutely sure that you have all of your ducks in a row. Consult with your business attorney, have them review everything. Schedule an inspection of the property if required. Don't let any of the red tape go unchecked.

2. Is the property clean?

There are many reasons why people walk out of stores or away from them without spending their money. Cleanliness, or lack of, is definitely one of those reasons and a problem that serious business owners and managers really should not allow.

Make sure, before you open your doors to customers, that you have thoroughly cleaned your gas station, including the areas outside and around the pumps. There shouldn't be garbage or any other form of clutter lying around the place.

3. Is everything stocked up?

After a few days in business, most customers will understand if you are out of something they want. There's really no excuse for being out of something when you have just opened. With all the talk of positioning yourself to engage your market, it is totally counterproductive actually to have a customer engaged then find that you actually can't follow through and give them what you want. Not only is that, but the fall out pretty bad. If you are out of something your customer has asked for, even if you manage to find a substitute, the customer is still going to walk out of your store with the impression that yours is not the store to go to for whatever it was they wanted that you didn't have.

4. **Do your staff members know their job, and are they ready to get started?**

As you will quickly learn, knowledgeable and motivated staff is going to be one of the most significant factors for the success of your business.

If your staff members know what they are doing or what they could be doing at any given time, if they are actually doing it, honestly, you are going to be fine. You will find yourself supported by a veritable army. You will be able to keep your ship in shape and running smoothly.

If, on the other hand, your staff members don't yet know their job or, worse, they are not all that motivated to work, you need to try and address these issues before you open the door.

Make sure you clearly outline the job responsibilities for each of your employees.

Make sure your employees have actually reviewed their job responsibilities and know that they must follow them as much as possible.

If motivation is a problem, make sure that you take some time, before opening your gas station, to have a meeting with your staff members and try to engage them with your company mission.

Be ready to find replacements if you are truly unable to get your team members motivated, but you shouldn't be having.

First Day Contingencies

Backup plans are not just sensible, they are imperative for a business to be successful, particularly in the long-term.

Something else to do before you open your doors is to make sure you have mapped out a worst-case scenario, a "what if this happens to us" plan. Try to cover as many eventualities as you can imagine.

Keep in mind, too, that the longer you are in business, the higher the probability that something will happen that requires the execution of a backup plan. It may be a minor issue or a series of minor issues. Few things in business come with guarantees except that you will, at some point, face an unexpected situation.

There are certain things you have to develop contingencies for. For instance, you have to have a plan if there is a fire or some other kind of serious event that puts people – yourself and your staff included – in danger.

You also need emergency plans for possible robberies or attempted robberies. How will you deal with those situations? You need to make an effort to ensure that your staff has the training to handle these events or at least know what to do and not do.

You should also consider the less serious problems such as what to do if there is something that you have run out of at the store or if there are issues with a customer.

Again, the more you can do to be prepared, the better. Think of as many eventualities as you can and plot plans to address them.

Establishing Your Daily Schedule

Granted, the first day of business, perhaps even the first week, is not necessarily going to go without any kinks. It's the nature of operations, the nature of the business.

You should, however, use the first few days of your business opening to gauge a schedule for yourself and for each member of your staff. Create checklists and make use of them. Make sure that your staff makes use of them.

It sounds unimaginative, but you and your staff will work much more effectively when there is a clear schedule and clearly designated responsibilities within that schedule.

For instance, you should have a schedule that includes timeframes for cleaning parts of the store. The cleaning activities should be incorporated in the main schedule, and you should give some specification about who is responsible for managing those activities and making sure they get done.

There should also be a schedule for taking stock, checking the inventory, and ordering any additional supplies.

Before you open the doors, take some time to review all of the things that need to be done within the store, breaking things down in terms of what needs to be done daily, what can be done every week, and what can be done less frequently.

With that, work out a schedule that you can follow from day one and make adjustments to as needed.

Promote Your Store With a Smile to Get People Through the Door

A typical convenience store carries on average about 2500 to 4000 unique items. We have talked a lot already about getting to know your market and working on your marketing data to figure out how you can engage your consumers.

Find what the store lacks and what your niche could, therefore, be. Find out what the niches are for your competitors, too. Knowing this will help you craft your brand that much more effectively.

For instance, if you notice that there are only handful gas stations in your area selling hot deli food, but none of them are in close proximity to your business then, you may have a ready market there.

Short to medium-term strategies for promoting your business are a little different but no less important. You should definitely have a grand opening and relevant specials when you open your doors. Keep in mind that you can repeat this promotional activity every couple of years, too, without doing any damage to your credibility.

Perhaps the best way to work out your market position is to apply a market attractiveness versus competitive position or SWOT analysis. Either one of these activities, completed correctly, will help you identify what you should emphasize to top your market.

The layout of the store is also going to be important and may require you thinking things out with some kind of visual. It's important to keep salty snacks close to the beer. Sweet cakes should be closer to the coffee area. Take some time to think about what foods tend to go together, and you should be able to work out where things should go, how people are going to be buying items, what items they are going to tend to buy together.

Another important strategy is the use of sensory stimulation. You should try to keep the store smelling of freshly baked cookies or similar because this will help to make customers hungry. If they are hungry, they will tend to buy on impulse.

Coffee and fountain soda can bring people if you do the right promotion with them, too, but that is something of a numbers game. During the summertime, offering a special (like .89 cents any drinks). During the winter, emphasize warm drinks, perhaps with a special of .79 cents for any size coffee.

Have a ready list of your high-profit-margin items and make sure that they are prominent within the store.

The biggest and fastest way to bring people through the door in a gas station is always that gas price ID sign that shows how much your gas prices are.

As part of your marketing plan, make sure you stay connected to the fluctuating gas prices and try to always offer the lowest price possible. You have to remember that pricing gas can be a very slippery slope. If you sell at a much lower price than your competitors, you may lose money.

On average, 80% of your gasoline sales are via credit card, and the credit card processing fees are around 1.75%, meaning you pay nearly 2 cents on every dollar you sell in gasoline. A gallon of gasoline sold via credit card at $3.50, you pay little over 6 pennies when most retailers only make around 7 to 10 cents a gallon gross profit. In this case after taking the credit card fees out of the gross profit, you may be left with 1 to 3 cents profit.

Chapter 11: Building Your Business Through Marketing

The key to effective marketing is to get into the mind of consumers. As bestselling author Orvel Ray Wilson once stated, "Clients buy for their reasons, not yours."

Identify the reasons people might be interested in what you are selling. Even before you open the doors to your business, you should be researching, talking with, and really listening to those who fall within your target demographic. Gather and analyze data from the feedback you are hearing and then use it to create a plan of action.

Now, all of this you have probably heard before and a marketing plan is not to be taken lightly by any business.

Part of the challenge of managing a gas station business is that you can probably get by and make money without doing all that much to rally the market or even actively upsell. At least, that's what some people think.

It's not to say that having a gas station business is not relatively easy as far as making a profit goes. Well, actually, it should be. With many business models like this one, people assume that there is a fixed scope for doing business, that there are well-established practices that really cannot be challenged. Wrong again.

Marketing and strategizing, actively selling to your customers is all that much more important in a gas station business than it is in any other business. Success will require ample consideration and dedication. An accountability partner might even need to be recruited to help plan your marketing strategy and ensure that you follow through.

Marketing plans might include decisions like where to advertise, whether coupons might be appropriate, a business name and logo, networking strategies, and service specialties.

Get a good foundation planned out initially, but keep in mind that your strategy can be adapted to your needs along the way. For instance, you might realize your website or brochures need more concise text because most of your clients are short on time. The most important goal you can achieve with effective marketing is identifying customer needs and filling those needs with your products or services.

But before you can get to the client to give feedback, you have to get them to like you, and this is where it can get a bit trickier. First impressions are everything, whether it's your business card, letterhead, e-mail, handshake, attire, office cleanliness, or the first 30 seconds of a phone conversation.

Rest assured your prospective clients are using their initial impression as the basis for an assumption about you and your business. This is why your entire appearance and persona must be professional from start to finish – otherwise, it can literally cost you money. The process of marketing does not have to be as complicated as it may seem. A fairly short list of considerations can have you on your way to expert marketing – and a growing client list – in no time!

Build Your Image

What image do you want clients to see? You can use your business name, motto, and logo to create a wide variety of images, from serious to silly. You need only make sure it is professional, and it fits with your industry.

Likewise, a playful logo or motto is fine for a clown company, but should probably be used sparingly in companies dealing with serious subjects like finances and legal issues.

There is one marketing principle that cannot be stressed enough. The best marketing efforts in the world will do you no good if you are inconsistent. Your website, business cards, brochures, flyers, and direct mailings should all have a similarity of appearance so clients can instantly recognize your company.

Even if you do decide to play around with the wording or spelling of your motto, or use a humorous logo, you can still project professionalism. How? Have your marketing materials professionally designed, or at least use high-quality photos, ink, and paper. To become successful, you must appear as you're already successful.

Diversify Your Efforts

There is no right way to market a gas station business. Instead, you should do what works best for you – and don't be afraid to get a little creative. You could do the normal tricks like advertising in local publications or ordering business cards and posting them around town. You could also make t-shirts, hats or bumper stickers, teach a community class in your area of expertise, or join the local Kiwanis, Rotary Club, or Chamber of Commerce. It might sound unusual, but this is how other businesses establish themselves and, if you are prepared to go really the extra mile with your business, then these strategies are perfectly viable for a gas station business too.

You might even consider renting a booth at a conference or expo show where your target demographic will be in attendance. Set up your exhibit and place a fishbowl to collect business cards for a drawing to win your product or service. At day's end, you get exposure for your business. If you even get to tell one person that your gas station is offering a particular promotion or that you are going to double-up and offer certain mechanical services, that you perhaps are going to maintain a carwash, or you are going to have someone on your lot to clean cars, then you have made the whole experience worthwhile putting yourself out there.

Take a variety of approaches to broaden your business and create exposure to the world.

Try to strike a balance between active and passive marketing activities, those that actively engage clients in the interaction and those that require no client response at all. Under the active marketing category, you might teach a workshop or class, cold-call, or ask clients for referrals.

Under the passive marketing category, you might post your business cards on bulletin boards around town, set up a website or distribute newsletters, update your gas price daily on apps like 'Gas Buddy' (https://www.gasbuddy.com/). These are all well-balanced approach to generating new clients, a never-ending process when you're an entrepreneur.

Under the active marketing category, include things like mini flyers about your upcoming sale on 12pk Soda or such and insert these in each of your shopping bags, so every customer gets one. If your city allows, you can put up some sales banner on the parking lot. But the most effective tool that is just coming to light lately is SOCIAL MEDIA

MARKETING. I know I typed it in all caps, I did so to bring your undivided attention to this new subject.

Now you may wonder what your Facebook has to do with your gas station business. Lately, Facebook, among other social media platforms is becoming the king of all marketing tools for small businesses.

The way I do it is I print out mini sales flyer with some type of sales, and at the bottom I say "Like us on Facebook and receive a $1 off coupon." It worked wonders for me, and you too should try it. The first month I started it, I gave out $756 worth of coupon, but in 3 months I increased my sales by 18%.

Social media is a very powerful tool, but only if you use it right.

Stay Organized and Diligent

Just like the best marketing plan in the world will do no good if you are inconsistent, it will also do no good if it never gets off the ground. Implementing and maintaining a marketing plan requires organization and diligence. Business could be booming one month and down significantly the next.

One of the reasons you need to create activity schedules and include marketing activities on them is that you really need to work to stay organized and diligent with your business. The more organized you are with everything from paperwork to marketing to the management of your store, the better you will survive, and the more you will thrive in your business.

Logos, Mottos, and Slogans

As you improve your sense of who your customers are, you will also get a better idea about how you can draw their attention to winning their business. Part of this drawing in the process will certainly touch upon your brand, the outward impression your business gives, not only of the services provided but of elements such as core values.

Some of the most important aspects of branding come together in the images and key phrases associated with your business. Think of GEICO and the gecko, Nike and their swoosh symbol, the Ritz Carlton and their slogan of "We are Ladies and Gentlemen serving Ladies and Gentlemen."

Unless you are the only gas station in your area, you are going to need something that differentiates you from the competition and something that people can recognize you by.

When you identify a logo for yourself, when you have a brand concept to work with, you should also make a point of incorporating it in as many different ways as possible. You may not need to have direct sales material, but you may find it useful to have a web presence. At the very least, list your business on Google Maps and other social media sites like FourSquare.

However you choose to showcase your gas station business, whether it is through signage outside your store, online, or in literature (like a menu, say) that you make available to customers, having an eye-catching, memorable logo and slogan will help ensure that customers remember you and become repeat customers.

The First 30 Seconds – What Sales Should Look Like In a Gas Station

Always keep in mind that the first thirty-seconds of contact are the most important thirty- seconds of the entire relationship. People live for first impressions, whether society cares to admit it or not. All of us are, at the core, superficial, even when we are buying gas.

Make sure your staff members and your business facilities look professional at all times. Make sure that you keep your business well stocked with everything you sell. Make sure, if you ask your patrons to pay at the counter, for instance, that there is always someone there.

As far as impressions go, what I have just mentioned is the tip of the iceberg and the kind of thing most people think about automatically. You and your business are not the only points of contact with new prospects but flagships for your company and for the business that you are trying to develop it into.

You have got to make that first impression count each time a customer steps into your store. That means following through on many of the things we have talked about. It also means being ready to think outside of the box when the occasion calls for it and when there is a need to go beyond the basics of sales to meet the needs of a customer and show them that you value their business.

Chapter 12: Hiring The Right People

At some point, probably quite shortly after establishing your business, you are going to need to hire staff to manage your facility. The more you realize you have things to do to keep your business operating at a profit, reaching its target audience, the more you know the value of having a staff you can rely on for job focus and dedication.

To make the process of hiring and managing staff as simple and as effective as possible, there are a few strategies you can employ to ensure that you hire the best people for the job and that you jump through all of the necessary hoops for your business to be in compliance with employment laws.

Establish systems to ensure that your employees know what is expected of them at all time. Accord the appropriate degree of respect for all things work-related. Honor your employees and let that be a guiding light for your behavior as an employer. As you prepare to hire your first employees, proceed with caution.

To commit to an employee's salary and benefits, you are making a costly commitment. When you are starting up, even though your gas station isn't your typical "start-up," you have to be particularly careful about making those commitments. Few start-ups can afford to have even one employee. That you can afford more than one (that you need more than one) isn't going to change the seriousness of the undertaking.

There's also the issue that firing an employee can not only result in severance pay but also, in some instances, possible litigation, with time and resources having to spend on finding a replacement.

The first issue you are going to have to address, as you process the issue of hiring, is where and how you go about finding good, reliable, and qualified candidates. To do this, you have to figure out what position to fill first. You have to consider the situation of your business.

You are also going to have to boil down your staffing plan to a handful of people who can get your business out in front of the people that matter. Consider that you are probably not going to be hiring your top salespeople right away, or even early on in the life of your gas station. Just as few high-level executives are not usually hired until a company has experienced some significant growth. You are going to want to concentrate your employment resources on finding people that can help you keep your business running or who can help you get it up and running.

You are also going to need to think, at least for a couple of positions, whether you actually need to hire a person for each of the positions you have listed. Do you need a sales clerk to work for each of the shifts you have outlined? Can you commit to working one of those shifts? Do you need to hire an accountant right off the bat or can you manage the books yourself for a couple of months as you figure things out?

To solve the problem of what you can outsource and what you need employees, consider the main strengths of your business. Identify where your weaknesses are in terms of managing the company, keeping up with the schedule of activities you have outlined for your business. With those things in mind, prioritize the positions to staff first.

When it comes to choosing a candidate, think about who is likely to be the best 'fit' within your new business environment. As we have said, you don't exactly have a start-up, but your gas station business probably has the vibe of something new, something vaguely experimental.

That being the case, you don't necessarily want to hire the person with the flashiest credentials. In fact, having someone who has tons of experience working in retail, for instance, or in a mainstream business environment may not be your best choice; they may not appreciate the need to be flexible, to think outside of the box, and even occasionally, to be unconventional.

A key selling point for working at your gas station will be the opportunity to work in a less bureaucratic environment. Your business should also offer an environment that is relatively rich in terms of opportunity. You are offering pretty high growth potential for most of your employees, assuming your business turns out to be the success you expect, the success you are planning for.

Because you are offering employees room to breathe and room to grow, offering this in exchange for their enthusiasm and their "get it done" attitude, you can focus on finding employees that are going to appreciate you as a leader as well.

Probably your best bet for finding reliable employees is networking.

Ask your family, friends, former colleagues, and advisors for suggestions.

Once you have your first few employees, then you can start to use them for referrals, so long as you continue to emphasize the need for only serious candidates to apply.

You can also explore job boards like Monster.com and your local newspapers. Craigslist is another potential site for recruitment, although you may want to go for job boards like and your local publications first.

Establish Job Descriptions and Positions

Figuring out what types of professionals you need and determining what those jobs are going to look like – it sounds straightforward until you try to do it. A lot of thought needs to go into your job descriptions and the particulars of the positions you create within your company.

Not only will job descriptions help ensure that your employees know exactly what is expected of them but putting together an effective description will also make it easier for you to find exactly the right type of professional to join your company.

If you think who you hire doesn't matter, consider this. Customer service is the cornerstone of any business success, including the success of a firmly brick-and-mortar business like a gas station.

You need qualified, capable people on the frontline of your company. You need them to be motivated, engaged, and functioning. These qualities are so much easier to find (and hold on to) if you manage to create a clear job description, communicating exactly what is required of individuals in any given position.

The first step to creating an effective job description is a job analysis. A written job description should involve first identifying the clear purpose of the position. If the job is being used to hire someone for a specific position, it will likely include everything from the job position title, a summary of the position, a list of responsibilities and duties, and the areas of authority and supervision outlined. It would also include a description of work conditions, qualifications required, and compensation to be provided.

If a job description were being used to outline an existing position, it would likely include most of these elements, except for the last three.

The job analysis should discuss the various attributes of each position. The best way to determine what these attributes are is simply to create a table or worksheet with key information.

The key information includes duties and responsibilities for each job, including what tasks will be performed, the type of decisions the person is going to make, and the responsibilities for record-keeping.

The second component covers qualifications desired for the work, including any information on physical abilities required, general skills needed, previous experience or special training required, or any specific knowledge or licenses.

Finally, the concept of the work environment should detail the location and work conditions under which the job is performed and supervisions and contacts with other business personnel, customers, and input suppliers.

Job design efforts should:

- Explain how the flow of work is going to be made efficient

- Whether more than one person may be capable of performing the job

- What you can do to make the work more rewarding

- Whether there is a way to organize work so that employees can manage to vary their activities according to personal needs

- Work habits

- Circumstances in the workplace

- Training programs that may help employees understand what they need

Once you have addressed the job analysis and job design components, you can create a specific job description.

The description should include:

- A title
- Job summary
- List of job tasks
- Responsibilities
- Authorities
- Job qualifications
- Proposals for supervision
- Work conditions
- Salary and benefit determinations

For your gas station, you may find that this varies according to the exact nature of the model you create. You are going to need to have at least two people available to work in the store as clerks during each day that you are open. You are also going to need at least one person to work a night shift unless you are planning on having closing hours.

You will have to think about the best way to break down the work hours.

Depending on your own availability, expertise, and how comfortable you are with skilled jobs, you may want to consider hiring a consultant for marketing and advertising campaigns.

You should also have an accountant and a lawyer on hand to work with your gas station business.

Calculating Wages and Benefits

Determining the wages and benefits to apply to each position, you are going to need, first, to consider the legal ramifications. You will have to look at the minimum wage requirements and other employment laws.

Once again, if you have an accountant, let him or her handle this part as this is really a component of the payroll service. The only part that you need input here is how much you would want to pay each of your employees. Once you decide that, they can handle the rest.

Creating Employee Applications and Contract Drafts

This sounds a lot harder than it actually is, and there are plenty of sample employee applications and contract drafts ("contract of employment" drafts) for reference.

First, the application should ask for general information on the prospective employee:

- Name

- Age

- Date of birth

- Social security number

- Work authorization in the US

- Address

- Phone number

- Education history

- Work history

- Specific qualifications

- References

It should also include a section for specific business equipment skills for certain jobs around your gas station such as experience handling gas pumps and performance of mechanical operations of cars.

Along with your employment application, the details for which are outlined above, you are going to need some form of statement to serve as an applicant selection criteria record, showing that your hiring selection process is going to be based on good-faith hiring practices.

The equal opportunity employer act's emphasis on gender equality, ethnic code, information on how selection criteria apply, and, once you have selected a candidate, the elements of your selection should be considered.

You are also going to need to have an application form waiver. A basic draft that can be quickly modified. You can establish authorization checks for credit, character, and reputation as needed. You can also include information about authorizing drug and alcohol testing.

The post-employment information form, the form you hand to the person you choose to work with, should cover exactly what you want to achieve, vital personal statistics that apply, a section to add information on who to notify in an emergency, information on dependents for insurance purposes, and a summary of job information, including job titles, rates, and methods of pay.

Visit my blog at http://www.gasstationbusiness101.com/ to download a sample job application I hand out at my stores, but please keep in mind that you may need to modify that based your state regulations.

Managing Your Staff

Managing your staff is about supporting your staff.

To provide exceptional customer service, you have to be prepared to support both your employees and your customers.

Recognize the importance of your customers and your employees, creating an environment in which they can work together effectively.

Learn to trust the judgment of your employees when you are faced with unreasonable customers. If you put employees first, they will be happy at work and better equipped to provide the highest quality of customer service.

Chapter 13: Understanding and Maximizing Sales

It is again something of a stretch to recognize that there is really an active, or perhaps we should say dynamic, sales process going on with your gas station business. The more research you do, the more you will piece together the elements of your competitors' sales and marketing programs.

Consider how many grocery stores, for instance, have 'to-go' convenience stores with gas stations attached, and how many of them implement customer rewards programs. In fact, most of the gas stations in the United States – most of the chains, anyway – institute customer rewards programs to entice consumers to, well, become loyal customers.

Exceptional customer service is a business issue, and businesses the world over are taking a closer look at how they address it. More than this, customer service is a strategy on the annual goal chart, a part of employee performance reviews, a focus group topic, and number one on the satisfaction survey.

Providing exceptional customer service means ensuring your customers are happy. Listen to what your customers want and need. Supply your finest service and ensure that it is provided on time. Provide prompt responses to all communications and inquiries.

Remember that manners matter. Whether an interaction involves dealing with a sale or dealing with a complaint, treat your customer very well. When customers complain, you should still be thanking them for bringing the problem to your attention. Always be present, polite, focused, and say thank you.

You are also going to need to keep your customers happy, adding value to your business and the service you provide. Look closely at the pricing of all of your products and services.

Do some pricing research. You need to work on loyalty versus customer satisfaction, and pricing research is one of the ways to do this. The other way comes down to providing exceptional service with each customer interaction, designed to create customer loyalty.

What does exceptional customer service amount to? First, it amounts to a smile on the face of every one of your employees. Teach everyone to smile. It's crucial. In today's fast-paced environment, a smile will make a huge difference.

Second, if you can, with as many of your repeat customers, learn their names. No matter what the business, customers love it when people know their names. Make that part of your agenda for your repeat customers.

Third, you should remind your staff to always be courteous, which basically involves using certain words and phrases with enthusiasm, including "please," "thank you," and "can I help you?"

You should encourage your staff to ask for customer feedback, too, and you should do it as part of the overall function of your organization, as part of your market and sales research.

In the bigger picture for customer service, you are also going to want to make sure that you and your staff work on maintaining a "service attitude." This is an attitude that basically reinforces the idea that you and your organization are there to help your customer, not simply to make money. Emphasize that you want to help your customers.

Ask specific questions. Ask, "On a scale of 1 to 10, how would you rate the service you received today?"

If you ever receive a low score, find out why. Tell your customers that you strive for a 10 and ask them what you could do differently to earn that 10.

As part of the sales dialog, your staff should also make a point of inviting customers back.

Make sure your staff knows to pay attention to the smallest details, responding to customers instead of reacting to them. You should still try to anticipate your customer's needs in the gas station business as if you were in a service business.

Be a leader yourself, in this, and hold yourself and your staff accountable for service delivery.

The more effectively you can master these steps, the better you and your staff will be able to implement policies for up-selling to your customers – selling more items than your customer came in to buy.

The layout of your store is going to play into this, and we have discussed some of the key points, like having the salty foods near the soda, the sweet foods near the coffee stands. For up-selling, your best bet is going to be your team and the level of customer service you provide.

Keeping Up Appearances

The appearance of your store is going to play into your customer service and sales experience, too. When I say appearance, I am talking about the overall outlook of the store. Does it carry a professional look?

If you are a branded store like Chevron, Shell, or BP, then the professional look of your store will easily carry over. You will likely have some uniform requirements to follow. If you are an unbranded store like "John's Quick Mart," you should still make sure your employees have some sort of dress code or uniform that they maintain.

There is also the smell and cleanliness of the store and the parking lot to factor in, both of which are factors that make a huge difference. Your dispensers should be clean. You should have window cleaners out by the pumps.

All of the card readers should be properly stocked with paper so your customers can get receipts without a hassle. The canopy of your store should also be well lit, and all the bulbs should be working. If there is landscaping to be done, it should be done with reasonable regularity.

All the gas nozzles and hoses should be in working condition, and you should check on this regularly. For safety, as well as to minimize cleanliness issues, you should check the hoses regularly to ensure that there are no visible cracks. Disaster can soon ensue if a hose bursts. It is important to inspect and replace the ones that have a sign of wear and tear.

Another area you definitely need to keep an eye on are the restrooms of your facility, including those used by your staff if they are separate from those used by customers.

The restrooms actually tell the real story of any store. If you have clean restrooms, the chances are good that your business is in great shape. But what do we mean by clean? Well, everything from the toilet facilities to the sinks and floors should be clean. Automatic air fresheners are also a great idea and can do wonders for a store, let alone the restroom areas.

Inventory Management

The process of counting, organizing, and managing the inventory of your organization is not exactly a glamorous concept, but effective inventory management goes a long way to maximizing profits and eliminating waste in your store.

A good owner can improve retail inventory management by hiring a great team and creating efficient processes, as we have already discussed. Another and often overlooked step is the incorporation of a regular review process.

Your retail inventory is everything in a store that is up for sale, distinguishing these items from retail assets, which include things like shelving, computers, and your actual gas station property.

Like most stores, gas stations make a profit because they buy merchandise and sell that merchandise for a higher price. A streamlining of retail inventory management processes allows an owner or manager to know what goods a store has and helps to ensure viable profit margins.

The key to successful retail inventory management is having a fool-proof inventory control system and a qualified manager who understands how to manage it.

The big picture is that you have to be able to keep track of a lot of different pieces of information, including order frequency of the most popular items in the store and inventory counts for whatever items you sell on your shelves.

If you find yourself having to manage your own store inventory, make sure you develop the habit of checking stock and taking stock incorporated into your primary schedule. You should also make sure that you have a list of the restocking policies and return policies for the items you sell. You should also try to keep a ready checklist that you can annotate and update for entry of information into your computer as needed.

Loss Prevention

Theft occurs one of two ways in a typical gas station store. One of the methods of theft is internal. The other is external. Can you guess which one costs the most?

If you guessed external (by customers), you would be wrong.

As I mentioned earlier, a bad hire can cost you a lot. Aside from the issues we have already mentioned – such as the potential for litigation if things really go downhill – a bad hire is going to be the person most likely to rob you. Not only will they rob you with stealing directly, as in taking money right out of the cash drawer, but stealing can also involve "sweetheart" deals as well.

Employees can also steel indirectly, giving their friends and family merchandise either for free or in exchange for a few pennies. The ones that charge pennies instead of giving merchandise away for free, they are the smart ones because they are hard to catch.

By charging a few pennies, they make it appear, on the store video cameras or even to other customers and employees, that they are ringing items correctly and actually processing a proper transaction.

How do you minimize theft, including the most destructive form of employee theft?

You will never be able to stop theft 100% of the time, making it a non-issue for your gas station. Even if you and your immediate family work the store, there will be some (maybe very little) external theft to deal with.

Every big company like Circle K or 7-11 has loss built into their accounting system because it has become an industry standard. On average, there will be 1% to 2% of sales walk out of the store. Keeping theft to a minimum is possible, but the goal is to not have it grow more than 2% year.

How do you do this?

The first step is to set up video surveillance. My recommendation is that you spend the money here and get a good one. See if you can have the ones that connect to your cash register and record each sale.

With this kind of system, you can go back and look at any employee. You can see how much they are charging for what item. This is the way you can catch that smart thief that sold his cousin a carton of cigarettes for .99 cents instead of $49.99.

Most stores set up cameras inside the store but not outside. My second suggestion is, especially if you do not have the budget for an external outdoor camera, install some dummy ones. You should also post some signs around the pump dispensers indicating to people that they are under video surveillance. This can help you deter many potential troublemakers.

Another tip to minimize external theft, in particular, is to make sure your parking lot, inside, and outside the store is well lit. This strategy definitely helps deter "drive-offs" that will cost you at the pump.

Monthly inventory counts can give you a clear picture every month if you are losing product from your store. It is very simple to figure out from two consecutive monthly inventory count reports.

A typical store's register is set up with product category department, like soda, cigarettes, tobacco, beer, and motor oil. The best way we keep inventory and books is by product category.

Let's take soda, for example. Let's say the inventory report was done May 31st. You had $7,000 worth of soda in the store. The new inventory report was done in June and says that you have $4,000 worth of soda product currently.

See how much you sold for June. Say you sold $12,000 of soda that month. Check how much you paid to all of your soda vendors (Coke, Pepsi) for June.

Now, this how the math should work:

> Beginning Inventory + Purchases (at Retail Cost) - Sales = Ending Inventory
>
> ($7,000 + $9,000) - $12,000 = $4,000

If your ending inventory is less than $3,800, for instance, it should be a red flag. Meaning there is theft going on. You should do the same math for each department and see how you are coming out.

Just remember to retail your invoice each day, too. When you buy at cost and sell at retail, for your inventory to match, you have to count all purchase at retail.

For example, you bought 10 cases of 20oz Coke at $15 per case.

Your invoice says you paid Coke $350.

Here is how it works: to retail out this invoice, each case has 24 bottles, and each retails for $1.19.

The math is:

Number of Cases x Number of Bottle per Case x Selling Price of Each Bottle

Or:

20 x 24 x 1.19 = $571.20

Two types of people conduct external theft: customers and vendors.

While certain thieves may come to your store and pocket a few pieces of candy, which, at the end of the day, may cost you $5 to $7 bucks, a vendor theft can really cost you 100 times that.

A vendor thief may show you the invoice that they brought in 50 cases of certain beer or soda and other products, but in reality, they only brought in 43 cases.

For inventory management and theft prevention, someone must check the vendor each time a delivery is received.

Make sure invoices match what is being brought into the store.

It is a good idea to install an alarm system, something called a "hold up button" with monitoring service.

The way the holdup button works is simple. If your cashier smells trouble and feels that they need to call the law enforcement for, she can simply press a hidden button under the register. No one will know, but it will dial the local police department and let them know there is trouble at our site.

Train employees to make eye contact with each customers walking into your store is always helpful, this lets any potential wrongdoers know that the cashier took a good look at them.

I also prefer to install an extra security camera monitor right above the cashier checkout stand. This way, everyone can see they are being recorded in color.

One important must-have of this business is making sure you have adequate insurance to cover yourself in the event of any disaster.

Having a commercial business owner policy (BOP) insurance will help you cover yourself as effectively as possible when it actually comes down to money.

Keeping the Books(Accounting)

You are doing everything right, by the book, but do you know if you are in the red or the black?

Maintaining the books is just as important as keeping products on your shelves to sell. The accounting for a c-store is simple, you keep a monthly tally of all the vendors you paid to buy your merchandise and gasoline, keep track of all your sales and all the expenses you occurred for that month.

The simple math is sales –purchase = gross profit

      Gross profit – All expenses = Net profit

There is a number of ways you can do accounting for your store. You can hire a bookkeeper to do your books then take it to an accountant to take care of your tax needs, or you can do all that by yourself if you are willing to spend 15 minutes a day.

You will need some type of accounting software. There are many good ones out there such as Quickbooks (https://quickbooks.intuit.com/)

Conclusions and Appendix

The process of starting and effectively managing a gas station is complex. Multiple layers impact the success of a gas station. Multiple steps are involved in the daily management of the business.

With this book, you have the basics – something more than the basics, in fact – to get you started and attain a firm grasp on your very own slice of the American dream.

And the American dream is very much what we are talking about when we explore the potential of a gas station business. Everything we have outlined in these pages – from the strategies and tips to find the right property, down to security and inventory management – all forge together to create a template for a successful business.

They create a template for the type of business that is not only highly likely to be successful from the very first, but also the type of business that has tremendous potential for growth and out-of-the-box thinking applied to enhance marketing and sales.

Gas station business ownership and management has been very rewarding for me, financially and on a personal and professional level.

As you prepare to embark on your own adventure in gas station ownership, I hope you find the information and advice with these pages to be useful to you. I have also included a sample business plan for a gas station to help you gauge what this important document might look like for your business.

Again, I wish you the best of luck and look forward to your questions and comments via the CStore Business Academy Website (http://gasstationbusiness101.com).

If this book as been of help to you, please consider leaving a review wherever you purchased the book. I would sincerely appreciate it.

Sample Business Plan

Executive Summary

Who We Are

John Doe, the CEO of this entity, is a very capable person and a veteran in this industry. He started in this field with a national chain Speedway. He worked for Speedway as an area supervisor for 8 years and left them in 2000 to start his own venture in this business. To this date, he successfully operated and sold 8 stores.

John Smith started in the grocery/C-store business right after college as his family-owned and operated a store in Miami. He has been successfully operating 2 stores for the last 14 years.

Start-Up Summary

The store we are looking to purchase is an existing Circle B store located at [ADDRESS]. The price of this location is $350,000 + inventory at cost at the day of closing. We will put down an earnest money deposit of $25,000.

We will put a down payment of an additional $50,000 towards the loan. We would like a commercial loan with preferably a fixed low-interest rate for around 7-9 years amortization.

Objectives

- To capture an increasing share of the local and commuter traffic passing through Broad Street.

- To offer our customers superior products, at an affordable price.

- To provide customer service that is second to none.

Financial Highlights by Year

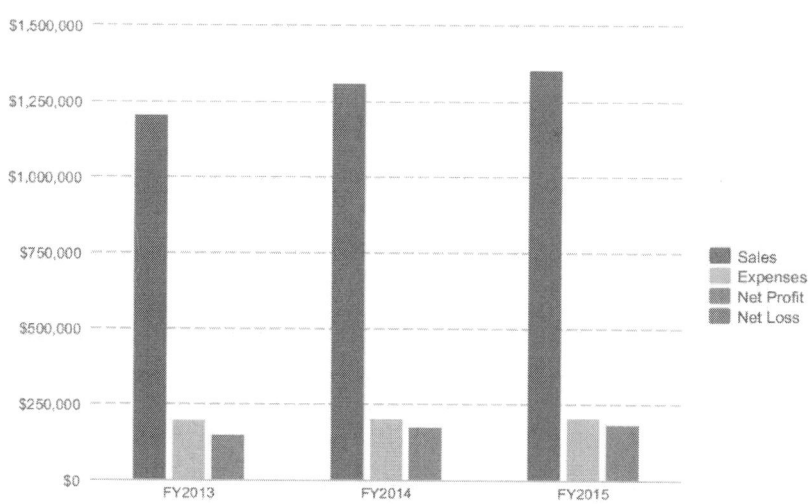

Company Overview

Delta Enterprise LLC was established in August 2012 to manage and operate gasoline service stations in the area. In August 2012, it successfully acquired and begun operating a Shell Oil location at 123 Main St.

John Doe and John Smith are the founder and owner of this limited liability entity. Both of whom have years of experience in owning and operating a gasoline service/convenience store businesses. Combined, they have over 30 years of experience in this industry.

The store will be managed and directed by John Doe, with seventeen years of experience in gas/C-store operations, and John Smith, an experienced retail food grocery store operator. John Doe will serve as the company's CEO and John Smith as the company's COO.

Delta Enterprise LLC is established as a limited liability company with 50% ownership by John Doe and 50% ownership by John Smith. The partners will share in management responsibilities with final decisions falling to John Doe, where there are differences of opinion. The partnership agreement allows for one partner to buy out the other in the case that the partnership must be dissolved and sets predetermined methods to calculate the company's valuation in that case.

Company History

This operating plan is for the Circle B store located at 456 1st Ave is part of Y's historic downtown and on the path of the beautiful yearly Mardi Gras parade route. This store has very steady sales figures over the years, and there are no other such stores in a 2-mile radius. This store is also surrounded by one of the largest government-subsidized housing projects in the city.

Management Team

This Circle B facility is a 24-hour store; it will require 7-8 hourly cashier/personnel and 2 supervisors. John Doe will be the acting store manager, and we will be supported by one assistant manager. The marketing, finance, and banking will be taken care of by John Smith.

The accounting and bookkeeping will be done by Jim Keck CPA PC, and all of the electronics, video cameras, and equipment will be monitored and serviced by Info Tech of Mobile Co.

SPS Pump Services will maintain all tanks, pumps, and all gasoline related instruments.

ELM Staff Leasing Co will provide the payroll service.

Products and Services

Below is a description of the products offered by our gas station:

Gasoline Sales

We expect to sell more than 350,000 gallons of fuel per year to motorists within the target market area. This is by far the largest revenue center for the business, but it does not generate an overwhelming amount of profit. The Company will use the gas sales as a primary vehicle for bringing people into the convenience store.

Food, Beverage, Merchandise Sales

The primary profit center of the Gas Station will be the retail sale of packaged food items, prepared food items, beverages (sodas, coffees, and bottled beverages), as well as other merchandise such as small toiletries, ancillary automotive merchandise (oil, fluids, ice scrapers, air fresheners, etc.). The Company will offer an expansive number of these items throughout the location.

Competitors

There is no immediate competition for our store. The nearest gasoline station is 2.2 miles away on the corner of X St and I-Y. In gasoline/grocery business, anything over 1.5 miles is considered a non-competition as people do not drive 2 miles to buy a pack of cigarette or for a gallon of milk. The store is surrounded by low to low middle-class neighborhoods, which is an ideal market for a C-store business and the strong sales figures provided by Circle B proves that theory.

Competition 1 - Chevron:

Chevron is considered a branded gasoline store where their wholesale fuel cost on average 2-3 cents more per gallon at wholesale level than the unbranded gasoline that we will sell at this location. This puts us at a much greater competitive advantage over the Chevron station.

Target Market

Market Overview

Our store's existing customers are divided into two groups as shown in the market analysis for zip code 12345

Group 1: 12,686 people who reside in 4804 homes in 12345 zip code are our local and immediate customers. The median income is $12,366. 76% of our customers are employed in construction, transportation, and service-oriented businesses.

Group 2: This group consists of all the downtown travelers and workers that travel on Broad street, a conservative estimate is around 22% of daily business does come from these travelers who like this store for its unique location as it is sitting next door to the only Church's Chicken in a 5-mile radius.

Market Needs

Our market is made up of consumers who have busy schedules, a desire for quality, convenience, and disposable income. They like a clean, fully stocked gas/convenience store where they can find cheaper gasoline compared to our competitors, reasonably priced beer, drinks, milk, and other food items along with friendly staff. They prefer a store that they can buy a gallon of milk even at 3 AM, as we are open 24 hours.

Marketing Plan

Overview

Our marketing strategy is a simple one: satisfied customers are our best marketing tool. When a customer leaves our business after purchasing a product, they know that they received the best price and service money can buy, our name and service will stand on its own via our cheaper process and very competitive gas prices.

In the retail gasoline business, the best advertising is the price pole sign that we have in the corner of our property, it has the power and ability to draw many hundreds of people a day into the store.

We intend to be very competitive and post at least 2 cents lower price on gasoline than our nearest Chevron branded competitor, which will draw enough of the travelers and locals into our store.

We will also run two cycles of promotions. In the summer we will promote fountain drinks, which have proven to be very successful in our industry. In winter, we will promote our hot beverages, like coffee and such.

Competitive Positioning

For local residents of 12345 who give us almost 80% of our daily business, we are the most visible and centrally located on Broad Street. We offer all the products an ideal station should carry at a very competitive price.

Pricing

Gasoline:

We will price our fuel at a cost plus pennies strategy and adjust it in every gas load delivered. All while keeping our competitor's price in mind.

Grocery:

We generally divide the C-store into 6 major categories, and the profit margins are usually as:

1. Cigarette at 22%

2. Beer/Wine at 25%

3. Tobacco at 32%

4. Soft drinks at 35%

5. Grocery at 37%

6. Automotive/oil at 40%

The average yearly gasoline margin historically has been around 9 cents/Gallon. The average C-store profit margin has been around 32%.

Promotion

As mentioned in the Overview, we intend to be very competitive and plan to do the following seasonal promotions for our store.

 *Buy"Fill up" 8 Gallons or more and get a Free Bag of Popcorn

 *Buy any 3 pack of Cigarettes and get a free lighter

 *Buy any size Fountain drinks for 89 cents (Summertime)

 *Buy any size of our Gourmet coffee for 79 cents (winter time)

 *Buy any 2-liter Coca Cola or Pepsi for 99 cents (Limited time offer)

 *Buy a combo Hot dog and any fountain drinks for only $1.59

There will be many more vendor-provided promotions year-round.

Financial Plan

Sales Forecast

	FY2013	FY2014	FY2015
	$1,204,000	$1,310,000	$1,350,000
Direct Cost			
Gasoline	$0	$0	$0
C-Store	$830,760	$903,900	$931,500
Total Direct Cost	**$830,760**	**$903,900**	**$931,500**
Gross Margin	$373,240	$406,100	$418,500
Gross Margin %	**31%**	**31%**	**31%**

Sales by Month

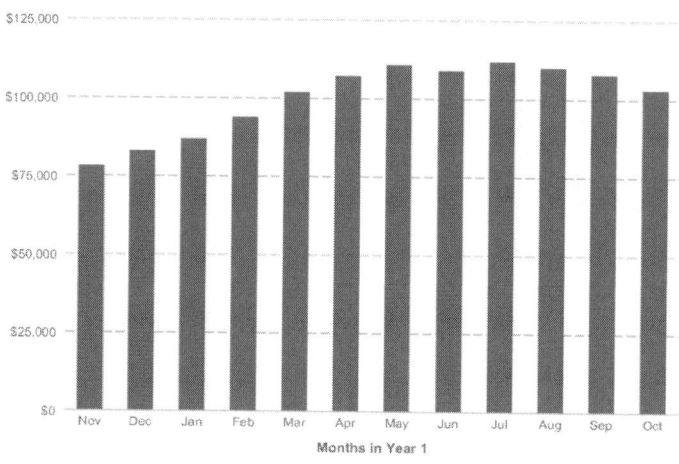

About the Sales Forecast

The gasoline sales forecast represents past historical data that Circle B provided us.

We showed very modest and minimal growth in next two years as the economy is still on a slow recovery, we anticipate this growth via our competitive pricing and better overall customer satisfaction.

Personnel Plan

Personnel Table

	FY2013	FY2014	FY2015
Store Manager	$31,000	$31,620	$32,252
Hourly Employee	$16,128	$16,608	$17,112
Hourly Employee	$16,080	$16,404	$16,728
Hourly Employee	$16,080	$16,404	$16,728
Hourly Employee	$19,800	$20,196	$20,604
Total	**$99,088**	**$101,232**	**$103,424**

About the Personnel Plan

This store will have one full-time store manager and 7-8 hourly employees. The store is open 24 hours a day, 365 days a year. So the store requires around the clock coverage. We forecast a weekly labor budget to be around $2,250.

Budget

Budget Table

	FY2013	FY2014	FY2015
Expenses			
Salary	$99,088	$101,232	$103,424
Employee Related Expenses	$11,892	$12,146	$12,402
Marketing & Promotion	$9,000	$9,000	$9,000
Mortgage	$36,000	$36,000	$36,000
Utilities	$33,600	$33,600	$33,600
Office Supplies	$900	$900	$900
Insurance	$7,800	$7,800	$7,800

| Total Expenses | $198,280 | $200,678 | $203,126 |

Expenses by Month

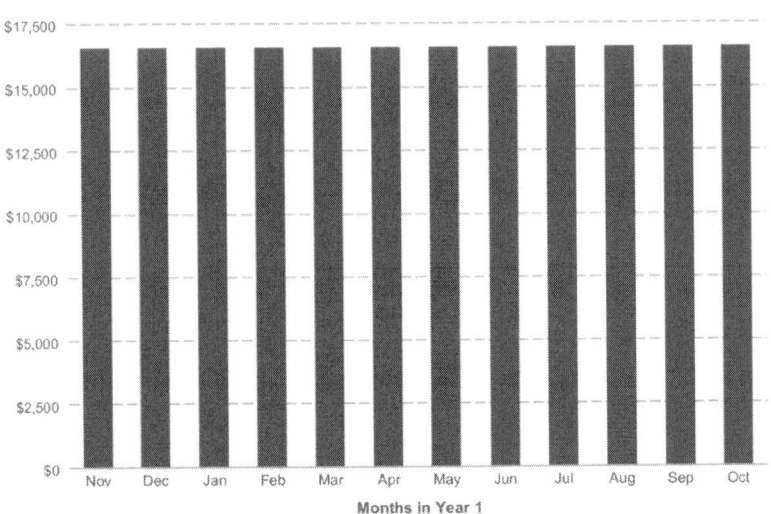

About the Budget

The Mortgage payment is based on a loan for $300,000. Insurance is based on similar payments for other stores we have operated. The utility and other expenses are all averaged yearly than divided into monthly payments.

Profit and Loss Statement

	FY2013	FY2014	FY2015
Revenue	$1,204,000	$1,310,000	$1,350,000
Direct Cost	$830,760	$903,900	$931,500
Gross Margin	$373,240	$406,100	$418,500
Gross Margin %	**31%**	**31%**	**31%**
Expenses			
Salary	$99,088	$101,232	$103,424
Employee Related Expenses	$11,892	$12,146	$12,402
Marketing & Promotion	$9,000	$9,000	$9,000
Mortgage	$36,000	$36,000	$36,000
Utilities	$33,600	$33,600	$33,600

Office Supplies	$900	$900	$900
Insurance	$7,800	$7,800	$7,800
Total Expenses	$198,280	$200,678	$203,126
Operating Income	$174,960	$205,422	$215,374
Income Taxes	$26,244	$30,813	$32,306
Net Profit	$148,716	$174,609	$183,068
Net Profit / Sales	12%	13%	14%

Gross Margin by Year

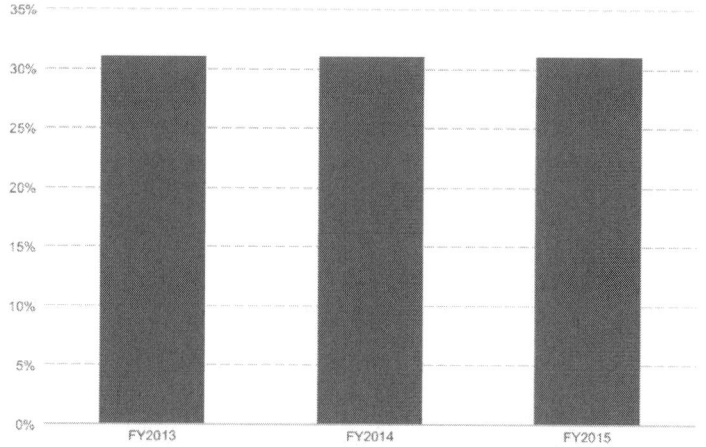

Net Profit (or Loss) by Year

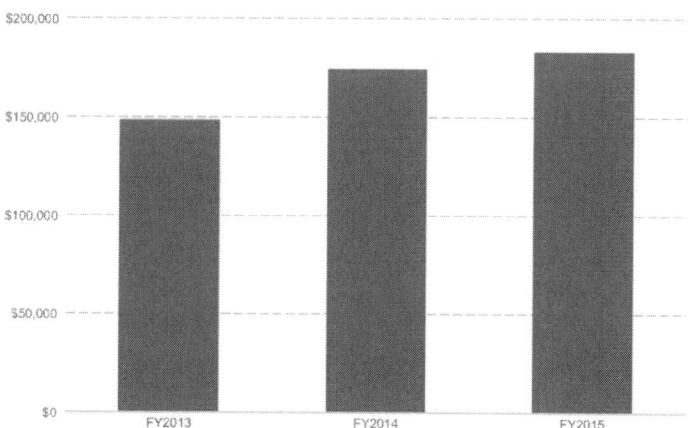

You can also download this business plan (in Word Format) from my blog at http://www.gasstationbusiness101.com/resources/.

Further Resources

In conjunction with reviewing this book, I recommend checking out my website, CStore Business Academy Website (http://gasstationbusiness101.com). You can also contact me with specific questions about your gas station business opportunities.

Lastly, as I mentioned at the beginning of the book, you can also listen to my free podcast on iTunes, Blubrry, Stitcher, and TuneIn Radio. Just do a search for Gas Station Business 101 Podcast.

Beyond this, there are several useful business books and websites you should consider checking out. These are just a handful of resources to use in conjunction with this book. While there are plenty more where these came from, in the interest of not overwhelming you, I have picked what I would consider among the most useful resources.

Some Useful Business Books

- *Beans: Four Principles for Running a Business in Good Times or Bad* by Leslie Yerkes

- *First, Break All the Rules: What the World's Greatest Managers Do Differently* by Marcus Buckingham

- *Getting More* by Stuart Diamond

- *Good to Great: Why Some Companies Make the Leap... and Others Don't* by Jim Collins

- *Love 'em or Lose 'em: Getting Good People to Stay* by Beverly L. Kaye

- *The One Minute Manager* by Ken Blanchard and Spencer Johnson

Some Useful Business Websites and Online Tools

- Evernote (http://evernote.com)

- IRS Website (http://www.irs.gov)

- Knowledge@Wharton (http://knowledge.wharton.upenn.edu)

- OnStartUps (http://onstartups.com)

- SCORE Website (http://www.score.org)

- Small Business Administration Website (http://www.sba.gov)

- U.S. Postal Service's Zip Code Lookup (http://zip4.usps.com/)

How to Start, Run, and Grow a Successful Gas Station Business

CSB Academy Publishing

ISBN: 978-0-9889478-0-1

Printed in Great Britain
by Amazon